ENLIGHTENED DEMOCRACY
Visions for a New Millennium

Volume One:
Introductory Essays
in

*Political-Economy,
Social Analysis
&
The State of the World*

J. Todd Ring

First Edition
Clear Light Publishing

ISBN: 1481074776
EAN-13: 9781481074773

⁂

"There is more day yet to dawn.
The sun is but a morning star."
– Henry David Thoreau

"Ours is not a caravan of despair."
– Rumi

"If you can imagine something, begin it.
Boldness has genius within it."
– Goethe

"If you have built castles in the air...
that is where they should be.
Now put the foundations under them."
– Henry David Thoreau

"If I can't dance, I don't want to be part of your revolution."
– Emma Goldman

TABLE *of* CONTENTS

FOREWORD

"The era of procrastination, of half-measures,
of soothing and baffling expedients, of delays is coming to its close.
In its place we are entering a period of consequences."
– Winston Churchill

To state what by now should be obvious to all, and which is increasingly undeniable to a growing majority, we must say this. Democracy is in peril. Liberty is in peril. The future of humanity on this earth is in peril. Justice, in all honesty, does not exist; and equality and peace are still dreams to be attained. For these reasons, this book has been written. I pray that it may be of some help to my fellow human beings at this critical time in our history. As the street-wise Yogi Berra put it, "It ain't over till it's over" – and I, for one, am not about to surrender.

The lives of our children, and all of the children in the world, ride now, on what we do or fail to do. Surrender is not an option. Despair is an understandable emotion, but it is not an option in terms of a protracted attitude toward the future. Inaction is not an option. Burying our heads in the sand is neither a responsible, nor a moral, nor even a sane option. Complacency is not an option. There is only one option, one choice, and that is the brave heart that lets love rule its actions, and follows the heart of courageous love into battle, with peace and non-violence, and into the streets and villages, towns and cities of the world, to begin the world again. We must now – as Thomas Paine urged two hundred years ago, *and we are here to complete the calling* – begin the world again. *For our children, we must begin the world anew.* There is no other choice. It must be done, and so it shall be done.

Just over two hundred years ago, the first wave of democratic revolutions broke out, to end the rule of feudalism and to institute democracy and the rule of the people, for the people, by the people. The trouble is: *we never finished the process.* Feudalism was never fully overcome or cast off, and it lingers on in new guises and disguises. *Democracy has not yet been fully born.* The task now is to finally and fully leave behind us the brutalities and injustices and the tyranny of the feudal era, and to make democracy real and full in its more complete and authentic flowering. There is no more essential or urgent task, for *all other positive changes that are necessary and that can be made, can only be made once real democracy is attained and power resides in the hands of the people, and not in the hands of a tiny ruling elite.*

Most people by now realize that there has been a corporate coup – that the corporate elite have taken over the political process. *There are many things that must be done to create a better world for all,* to create a more just, noble, peaceful and sustainable world, *but nothing can be done so long as our democracy remains hijacked by a corporate and financial elite. The first thing that must be done, therefore, is to reclaim our democracy.* Nothing is attainable until that first step is complete, and there is no point in our fooling ourselves that it might somehow be otherwise. Step one is the reclaiming of democracy by the people. If we fail at that, we have failed at everything. On this, the future of humanity depends.

The tide is changing now. A global democracy movement has sprung up in countries around the world, in over 1,000 cities. This is the time to make the changes needed. This is the time to act, to unite, and to reclaim our democracy, before we are taken into a very dark age of global neo-feudal corporatism. Now is the time.

The "Leave It to Beaver" era of cheerful servility to corporate power is over. Everybody knows the deal is rotten. Everyone knows the emperor has no clothes. Everybody knows that the corporate and financial elite pull the strings that manipulate our political and electoral process, as well as the media and the global economy. Everybody knows a silent corporate coup has taken place. But few dare yet to speak about it. We are in shell shock, in disbelief. There is a pervasive deer-in-the-headlights, stunned state of shock in our society as we slowly begin to come to terms with the fact that our democracy has been hijacked. But this too shall pass.

The state of paralyzed shock will pass, and when it does, as it is passing now, the paralysis and denial will give way to a powerful uprising of the people, who will demand their democracy back, and will actively reclaim it. This is what has now begun.

It is in our interests to avoid further denial or paralysis, if we have succumbed to these, for both denial and the paralysis of fear are extremely dangerous now – this cannot be emphasized enough.

It is in our interests to begin, if we have not already, to join the movement for the renewal and the reclaiming of our democracy. This is what must happen if humanity is to have a decent and bright future, or even, any future at all.

We must act, and act now. The time is upon us. Humanity is awakening. A new renaissance has begun. But first will come democratic revolution. And upon this, I assure you, the future of humanity depends. We cannot fail. We will not fail. United, humanity *will* see a new and better day.

JTR
November 15, 2011

INTRODUCTION

THE BOOK YOU HOLD is about values and visions. It is about the values of democracy, liberty, equality and solidarity; the values of compassion, dignity and peace, and of ecological sustainability. And it is about a vision for preserving, protecting, safeguarding and renewing these values, and for carrying them to a higher level than we have seen yet in human history. This is within our capacity. This is within our reach. And this is the project, the task of our time. It begins with a renewal of democracy. And the renewal of democracy begins with a profound and honest reflection and re-examination of where we stand, where we have been, what we value, where we are currently headed, and what direction we wish for humanity in the coming decades and centuries that hopefully lie before us.

As to commonalities and kindred spirits, intellectual heritage or common themes, this work is far more in sympathy with the basic clarity of Coleridge, Kropotkin, Bookchin, Bertrand Russell, Socrates and Spinoza, than with the slithering self-deceit of Spencer or Machiavelli; more in accord with the frank and stark, unflinching self-honesty of T.S. Eliot, Oliver Goldsmith, Goya or Dickens, than with the numberless apologists for power and their unwitting allies – the plethora of pangloss Pollyannas; more with Plato's parable of the cave (which rang true to my marrow the first time I read it, and was later confirmed with experience more empirical and direct than that of the most ardent fan of Newton) – far more than with Plato's ideal of the philosopher kings – certainly far more than with the polysyllabic platherings of the new Sophists, who now go by the name post-modernists; more with Asoka and Nagarjuna than with Alexander or

Aristotle; more with Martin Luther King Jr. than with Che; with Moyers over Murdoch, and Frieri over Freud or Foucault; with Schumacher, Suzuki, Daly and Cobb over Davos, or the lunatic empire-mongers at the Bilderberg club; with Joseph Campbell, Alan Watts and Thomas Merton, St. Francis and John Ball over Cromwell, or Constantine, Justinian or Savonarola; with Orwell, Huxley and Chomsky, Weber, Fromm or Sorokin, Shelley, Solomon or Heraclitus, over the breezy imperial platitudes of a Brzezinski or a Fukuyama; far more with Emerson, Whitman or Thoreau than with that consummate purveyor of illusions who is Hobbes; with Thomas Paine over Milton Friedman, and much more with Jefferson than Marx or Smith – to mention here a few kindred from the West, and but two from the East.

But names and labels cannot do justice ever to thoughts, and so reflection is much needed, of course. Let us remember that cookie cutters are for cookies: it is intellectually numbing to form an opinion based upon labels, pigeonholes and associations, rather than upon hearing and reflecting upon what a person actually has to say.

Let truth be all we revere, and save the deification for that which is beyond all words to describe. If we wish for enthusiasm or a rallying round virtue, let these come from our passion for truth, justice, democracy and freedom, and nothing more – that is, nothing less. *An individual may announce a moment in history, but never defines it: the people define their own history, always, whether by action or by default.*

Nevertheless, if you want a quick handle on the book, a brief letter of introduction so to speak – and it is hoped that this will spark thought and reflection, rather than preclude it – the work could be described as a populist democratic treatise on the now urgently needed renewal of democracy, and the philosophical foundations which must be entailed for this to arise and to be carried through to successful completion – as I believe it will, and quite soon at that.

In a nutshell, the book is a clarification of our present and past; a reassertion of the founding values of the Enlightenment and of democracy; and a grounding of the Enlightenment values of liberty, equality and solidarity in the perennial wisdom of humanity.

The subject matter is broad and deep, as well as extremely relevant to this moment in human history, and the presentation is, it is hoped, accessible to a broad readership. The objectives of the work are to clarify where we stand as human beings in this world at this time, at the dawn of the 21st century; and to crystallize the values, principles and awareness we will need to move through this century and beyond, with confidence, inspiration, boldness and vision. In short, it is an encapsulation of five thousand years of human experience and learning: an overview of what we need to know in order to survive, and to thrive, in the coming decades and centuries ahead.

The essays contained in the first two volumes are an introduction to the terrain covered by the following volumes, and span the range of subjects from philosophy to social and political theory, to contemporary social and political analysis and action, touching of necessity also on the subjects of science, spirituality, history, anthropology, psychology, sociology and economics.

For some, the more philosophical essays will be more to their taste or inclination; to others, the political: but I would urge the reader to read both, for they complement one another and build upon one another. Neither is complete without the other.

It could be said that philosophy and politics, when they are practiced with virtue and integrity – words that are rarely used today, and even less often practiced – represent wisdom and compassion, respectively.

Philosophy, when it is not an intellectual parlour game of egos and empty jargon, is the love of wisdom. (Yes, post-modernism has been thoroughly rejected here; and thankfully, after a forty-year sabbatical from our senses, it is dead in any case.) Politics is the life of the community, and when practiced with virtue and integrity, it is the expression of love and compassion. These may sound like overly idealistic terms to use in today's highly jaded, cynical and disillusioned society, but I would contend that if we do not reclaim these words, and more importantly, their meaning and practice, then we are lost – and not only as individuals or communities or nations, but even as a species.

Survival, as well as justice and well-being for all, by now recquires above all a rededication to the values of truth and love. These have always been the guiding values of our better sides and our better moments, and at this time, they have become truly critical.

We need not be afraid that speaking of truth, wisdom, compassion or love is to be overly sentimental or fuzzy-headed. Our greatest of leaders, such as Martin Luther King Jr., the Dalai Lama and Ghandi, have always spoken to these values directly or indirectly, and have tried to rekindle them within us and within our communities and society. We need them now more than ever. And it is a very clear-eyed and unflinching assessment of the situation at hand, as well as the sweep of human history, that brings us to that conclusion.

Philosophy and politics have been separated and divorced for some time now. We have mistaken the division of church and state for a division between philosophy and politics; and while the former is a wise precaution, the latter is a folly, and a disaster waiting to happen. In fact, the division between philosophy and politics has been a major part of the unfolding disaster which has been the past 100 years, as we race towards self-annihilation, with wisdom and compassion both largely divorced from politics, and philosophy shelved in some dusty tower off in some nook we have long forgotten about, to be pursued by dull bookish people while the world runs giddily and blindly toward self-annihilation.

Philosophy, if practiced with a basic and natural intelligence and a common sense which we all possess, does bring us a remembrance of our basic clarity of mind, and therefore grounds us in the real. Politics we cannot escape unless we seek to escape society – and even then, society will affect us, no matter where we run. Philosophy, in its essential sense, is a necessity for an informed and clear mind, or an informed and clear-minded society, whatever form that philosophical reflection may take. Politics is simply unavoidable – at least, that is, if we do not wish to be blind-sided either by tyranny, brutal injustice, or self-destructive patterns not of our choosing. If politics and philosophy are divorced, then the former becomes blind, while the latter becomes impotent.

Philosophy can and should guide and inform, ennoble, uplift and also ground our politics firmly in a basic clarity of mind and awareness as to what is real and what is wise. Politics in turn is the application of our philosophy in the realm of society. No man is an island. To ignore the political is not only irresponsible to our fellow human beings, it is also greatly unwise.

If we ignore the philosophical, then chances are our politics will be shallow and misguided, if not self-defeating, short-sighted, blind or disastrous. Politics divorced from philosophy is politics with an unconscious philosophy, and unconscious philosophy tends to be bad philosophy, for it is riddled with unexamined assumptions that may prove to be ruinous to all we are attempting to accomplish.

Unexamined assumptions are the minefield of our existence. If we wish to live well and live wisely, we will unearth every hidden assumption we can find, and put it to a serious and rigorous examination as to its validity, so that we will not be blind-sided and perhaps completely sunk by the erroneous and mistaken assumptions we failed to question or even to recognize. This means that we must be reflective, we must be philosophical. If we are not, then we are drifting, or racing, blindly in the night, with perilous shoals all around, and no radar, no night vision, nothing but dumb luck. This is no way to live. Neither is it any way to collectively steer the unfolding course of humanity. Reflection and philosophy are essential to a clear-eyed and wakeful, wise life, be it at the level of the individual, the community, or the society. *Politics and philosophy cannot be divorced without disaster ensuing.*

If we ignore the political, then our philosophy is likely to be largely useless, for we have alienated and estranged ourselves to a very considerable degree from the life of the larger community – and we are in this way neglectful of our duties to our fellow human beings and other living beings on this earth, for we are living in our own little bubble or shell, and it is only a rather callous shrug of the shoulders that can lead us to such a state of neglect.

Moreover, if we neglect society and the political, not only will we abandon others to struggle on without our help, but we will also be affected by that same society which we have abandoned, and that neglect will in all likelihood, sooner or later come to bite us on the ass.

The loner in the corner who thinks his cache of rice and beans – or champagne and caviar – will save him while he neglects the fate of the larger society of which he is a part, will be in for a rude surprise I am afraid, for no man is an island, and we are all in this together.

And a yoga mat and meditation cushion aren't going to save your skin if we allow human society to further devolve into a brutal and stark neo-Dickensian order that is rapidly making life anywhere impossibly harsh and toxic, on both a social and an ecological level.

We are forced to act, as well as to reflect. Action without reflection is blind. Reflection without action is either corrupt, or at least callous – or simply impotent and useless. We need both action and reflection. And we need them now. In spades.

If we are principally focused on the philosophical or spiritual, that is fine, but we cannot ignore the social and political, for humanity and living beings on this earth need us now. If we are principally focused on the political and the issues of society, then we must, if we are wise, look carefully into and reflect deeply upon the philosophical, lest our actions and efforts be self-defeating, unbeknownst to us, and we either waste our efforts, diminish their effectiveness, or else shoot ourselves in the foot, and cause more harm than good.

We need both a philosophical and a social-political re-examination of things, including our deepest and most cherished convictions and assumptions. These essays are intended primarily to loosen the soil: to broaden, deepen and enliven the dialogue, and to spark a deeper reflection, so that a freshness of awareness can blossom and grow naturally. It is our own basic clarity of mind, rediscovered or reasserted, that will save us now. From this, all that is positive will proceed.

Read both the philosophical and the political essays, and reflect on both, I urge you. One or the other may be more familiar or more comfortable, but this will change with exposure and time. Immersion is the way to give it our all. Dive in. This world needs our help, and we are at a crossroads.

So let us begin. Or begin anew. The past is a fading mirage, a passing dream. The future is not yet made. And the present is wide open. Our future is in our hands. So, too, the future of all of the children of this earth. Let us bring to this decisive moment all that is our best.

JTR
November 15, 2011

Post-script:

Two notes on major theses in the book:

1. The critique of puritanism presented here bridges pure philosophy and political theory, or the inner realm of consciousness and the outer realm of human society – it is one very important bridge among others. The recognition of the interdependence, unity and sacredness of life and living beings, which is presented and argued for here, is the recognition of the true nature of being, and this recognition of the nature of being brings us naturally to a valuing of life and a respect, appreciation, friendliness and compassion for all living beings, which in turn is the only attitude with which human civilization at this juncture can be sustained, much less function wisely, justly or well. Puritanism is both a symbol and also a cause or component of the pervasive modern and post-modern pandemic of pathological fear, mistrust and contempt for life, nature and human beings which runs directly counter to this re-awakened awareness of the unity, interdependence, preciousness and sacredness of life and living beings; and so, must be eradicated from the mind, as all illusions must be transcended and dissolved, so that we may live in basic clarity of mind, and hence, from this, in basic justice, well-being and peace. And the case is made in a straight-forward, accessible, almost conversational style, by the way, as is the general style of the writing throughout the book – so there should be no worries about dry, overly arcane, wordy jingo that hides more than it reveals. Again, it is a work for the intelligent layman, and not only the specialists in philosophy, politics or social theory. (This summary of two theses is much more challenging and less accessible than the book itself. Concision is often that way.)

2. To express it in academic terms, the main thesis which is put forward here is an ontological and empirical foundation for Kant's categorical imperative: a grounding in a purely empirical epistemological and phenomenological analysis of the nature of mind and being, and not in mere speculation or pure reason alone, of an ethical concept which

may intuitively inspire, but which is frequently held to be ungrounded or unsupported. Put otherwise, an empirical and ontological grounding is provided for the instinctive common sense of humanity, which is the golden rule of love of one's neighbour, so that the universal and central value of the world's religions, which is love, and also the Enlightenment values of solidarity, mutual aid, liberty, democracy and well-being for all, will have a foundation worthy and fully supporting of their wisdom and merit – so that in turn, our basic and natural instincts towards human sympathy and mutual aid, cooperation and compassion, are not overruled by a mind or a society that does not understand that these values are in truth grounded in a valid and accurate recognition of the nature of being – that, *to put it most succinctly, love is enlightened self-interest, based on the nature of existence.* From my awareness, such a foundation for a unifying set of human values has not yet been achieved, and is much needed – in fact, urgently needed, if humanity is to survive this present century. (Post-modernism is dead and is in any case a dead end, and Western philosophy is at an impasse. I am suggesting here a way forward – boldly, I admit.) In short, the major original component, and most essential element of this work of synthesis, is a grounding of post-industrial, 21st century values – Enlightenment values, as well as the universal and central value of all of the world's religions, the value of love and compassion – in a reawakened awareness of the fundamental nature of being, as supported by a radically empirical examination of being and mind, and by the corroborating voices of a rather slow but rapidly catching up science, as well as by the perennial wisdom of humanity. The polis and the ground of being are thus re-acquainted – as Plato attempted to accomplish, but without the elitist fantasies, and with a firm grounding in and of democracy instead. Politics and philosophy are thus reunited, and a comprehensive vision for the 21st century and beyond is presented for the consideration of the reader and the global human village. May it be of some benefit now.

JTR
December 14, 2011

AUTHOR'S NOTE

"If I am to be called a drum major,
then let it be said that I was a drum major for justice."
– Martin Luther King Jr.

"If I cannot hope to have pleased all sides,
I can at least suppose that I have in different places
displeased them all equally."
– G.R. Elton

W E NEED A NEW wave of salons, as in the days preceding the
French Revolution, when small gatherings of people met in coffee shops to discuss what mattered to them, and as a result, major
social change was born. Such informal discussions had such political power
that King Louis IV tried to ban coffee houses, the centres of political discussion, as did King Charles II of England in the 17th century. Conversation,
at least when it is free-spirited and thoughtful, leads to reflection, the clearing of the air and also the mind, and for these reasons also, not infrequently,
to the questioning, challenging, subversion and overturning of illegitimate,
unjust or oppressive orders and , therefore, should be engaged in more freely
and more often. Go to your favourite coffee shop, tavern or pub – drink decaf,
juice or water if you don't like alcohol or caffeine, and talk with people! Break
the ice and the silence, and let's get this party started! There is much we need
to discuss.

We need a new wave or a *new spark* of dialogue and discussion, or a new freshness to it. We also need a renewed reflectivity that precedes, accompanies and is the result of a new wave of dialogue. To these aims, this work is dedicated. Lest this goal seem mundane to some, let me elaborate a moment.

We often shy away from such questions when relating with others, as, "What is your philosophy on life?" Maybe we are too embarrassed that ours is underdeveloped or highly uncertain, or maybe we are afraid of bringing up possibly difficult, thorny or even divisive subjects, or maybe we have simply grown accustomed to a hyperactive mode of relating, in which serious discussion is hard to even initiate – amidst the text messages, phone calls and other myriad distractions – for there is no time, or no focus, or perhaps no courage or no heart, for such a thing as an unhurried, thoughtful conversation. Sound bites and nearly universal, epidemic ADD will have to do in this frenetic, superficial, hyper-distracted and scattered age, we may unconsciously conclude as we find ourselves drifting with the numbing tide. We may also shy away from philosophical questions when we are alone, in our thoughts or readings, for similar or other reasons. And our lives as well as our conversations, I would suggest, and indeed our world, suffers for it, if that is the case and we avoid our depths.

Likewise, we often shy away from broaching political subjects with others, unless we are sure we can do so without too much fuss or conflict. It is often said that the two things you should never talk about are politics and religion – and philosophy is on too dangerous a ground, along with religion, for many people as well. But if we can't talk about politics, then we can't talk about the polis, the larger community – which means, we can't talk about what is going on in the world, or what we should do about it, if anything. And if we can't talk about religion, spirituality or even philosophy, then we can't talk about the questions of values, questions as to the nature of life, the universe or existence, or about what is meaningful, worthwhile or even true.

In short, if we can't talk about politics and philosophy, we are thus preventing ourselves from talking about the things that matter most. This is a shame, on the personal level; and on the social or political level, it is nothing short of a disaster. Sometimes, there is no possibility at the present moment for meaningful communication on certain subjects, but often, we despair or shy away when we needn't do so; and our conversations and relations, as well as our lives, are the poorer for it. At the same time, if we shy away from subjects of politics, social issues or philosophy in our lives, thoughts, reading and reflection, then we are surely missing some important food for thought, avoiding some issues that in truth likely demand and require our attention, and steering clear of some very important, and potentially helpful, even liberating thoughts and ideas. We must engage with philosophy and with the world in which we live if we want a full and meaningful, rich or ethical life. Since many are interested in such subjects, yet many steer clear of them, I thought it may be of some help to put out this simple plea for the subject matter of politics and philosophy, in both our discussions, and in our lives. But this note was intended to state something else, so I will go on to that original thought.

After 28 years of study, many thousands of hours of research, reflection, discussion and meditation, and 12 years of writing, when it is now finally time to release a work that is hopefully of some help to this very troubled world, I must admit that I have serious reservations. I do not wish to offend or to upset, or to cause any undue distress or hardship for anyone, and I am tempted to tone down the tone of the book, so as to be more pleasing and soothing, and less biting, intense, or cutting – but that, I feel, would be unwise, if not simply irresponsible, for the situation we are facing collectively, and individually, is dire, and there simply is no room for the mincing of words. I am sorry for this. Please accept my sincere apologies in advance for any hurt or offended feelings. The intent was and is, to liberate through the power of clarity: which means, to cut through every illusion in order to liberate our natural and innate clarity of mind and common sense. Common sense has become, unfortunately, and even tragically, uncommon; but this is a temporary aberration in our human society, and one that can, and will be overcome, I promise you.

Every major obstacle that lies between ourselves and the future that we need to create if we are to survive as a species, and also to live decently, even richly – if we are courageous enough to make the needed actions, and do so without hesitation or delay – every major obstacle has been demolished, to the extent of my present awareness, as best it could be, by the power of the word, so that at least our minds may be free, or as free and clear as presently possible, and following that, we can begin to bring the rest of our being and our world to follow suit and complete the work.

In other words, the illusions that stand between our present situation and a new renaissance have been laid to waste using every power available, and to every extent possible, so that humanity may live, may survive, and may live well. History will show whether we succeed or fail. If we are extinct in fifty to a hundred years, history will have recorded our dismal failure as a grand and pathetic, moaning silence. Pray that we are not such fools. I, for one, do not believe we are, or I would not have spent the better part of my life devoted to research, reflection and writing for the sake of social change and transformation. We are not dead yet. Nor should we act so.

Better to beat a dead horse than to be one; but in any case, we are not yet dead, and only the dead of spirit can give into despair – inaction is unconscionable: despair is therefore not an option.

If it takes an air raid siren to wake us from our slumber as our world burns, then a siren *will be* sounded. If you are not alarmed, then you are sleep-walking, and you will be roused sooner or later by reality itself. Be not offended by those who seek to wake you before the warned of dangers arrive. Be offended by the tendency to self-numbing and paralysis, for this is what truly degrades and threatens us now, more than ever before.

Some may think the writing sounds arrogant, but extreme confidence is often mistaken for arrogance. Similarly, the use of certain words may be perceived as pretentious or showy, but the words chosen here are chosen not for show, but for precision of meaning or power of impact. Functionality of communication is the point, and the entire point. You don't use a finishing hammer for chiselling stone, nor do you use a masonry hammer for fine woodwork – words are like tools: if you only know how to use a couple, then your craftsmanship, that is, your skill at communicating effectively, is severely limited. You don't collect tools for the sake of showing them off, but for the sake of building something useful or beautiful for others to enjoy. It is the same with words and writing. They are tools of communication, and we shouldn't get too hung up on them.

I would also say here that I agree with most of what Chomsky has said, including this: "I don't believe in false modesty – I'm good at some things, and not good at others." We all have our strengths and weaknesses, and that has nothing to do with superiority or inferiority, and ego should not enter into it. In any case, arrogance is a belief in the superiority of oneself over others, and all such notions are delusional, as are all notions of inferiority, for Being is one, as Spinoza, Emerson, Thoreau, Whitman and countless others have realized, and duality an illusion. Our nature is basically good, and we are one, whether we are aware of the fact or not.

What matters is whether the work has a positive effect in the world, in human lives, and on human civilization, and *nothing* other. Form is emptiness; emptiness is form – this is not theory or conjecture, mere speculation or hypothesis, but empirically verified and first-hand corroborated fact. The messenger is empty. The form of the message matters only to the extent that it conveys the message. The finger pointing to the moon is not the moon itself. Cling not to form. See what is pointed out. I am certainly far from fully enlightened, but only a student and fellow traveller; but there is a hope and a confidence that these reflections and meditations can be of some help. I pray this is true.

The message is simple, though its import is routinely underestimated, and its implications are almost universally avoided: life is precious, and compassion is essential to a good life, an intelligent life, and to a good society, or even a viable society. The further details of the elaboration and the implications are set out here, and not with the gentle brush strokes of a wilted piece of limp leaf lettuce, but with the boldness and vigour the subject demands.

I could see no other way to write than with utter frankness, and with great passion, given the situation humanity is now facing. I still feel the same way. I am by nature quite soft-spoken and reserved, generally speaking, and I do not at all like to make people uncomfortable, nor to unduly ruffle their feathers, but would much rather have peace and tranquility among us. In fact, I am more likely to pass over minor problems, and often major ones, in silence, in favour of keeping the peace and not making a great fuss, rather than to say anything that may injure another's feelings or wound their pride, or sow or exacerbate any actual or potential division or conflict among us. However, there is a time for candour, and that time, I believe, has certainly come.

There are issues facing the human family – and we are one family, by the way – which can no longer be avoided. To avoid them now, or even to speak of them in less than fully honest, frank and even piercing terms, would be, I believe, an act of gross negligence beyond all description. Therefore, frankness and a ferocity of passion for truth and for justice, and for the well-being of all human beings and all living beings in this world, is in order, and is not held back. There are no punches pulled here, no excuses made or accepted, and nothing is sugar coated or dumbed down. It is raw, and it is real. Compassion is the underlying and overarching value, but compassion requires firmness and strength at times, and at times, the roar of a lion. If we insist upon being sheep, then we are all dead, both spiritually and also literally; and worse, our children have no future. This is unacceptable. Courage and passion and heart are now required of us all. We have run out of time for excuses, escapism, or waiting passively, hand-wringing, for someone to come and save us. It is up to us to fix the mess we are in, the mess we have gotten ourselves into, *and it is time* – and we have everything that we need to complete the task with success and honour and pride, before it is too late.

Even if we were not up against a wall, or peering over a cliff, whereby our very existence as a species is in question, which it is; and the future of our dear children, and their children, was not hanging by a very thin thread, I would still have to speak with the greatest of clarity, and at times, with intense passion and all of the power I can muster, for we are living in a truly diabolical state of the world. When the numbing paralysis of mind and body and soul that is induced by the daily spin and white noise of the media wears off for a moment, if it ever blessedly does for some of us at least, we can see with all the clarity that is needed, and with no room for denial, that the world is unjust in an obscene and extreme degree, and there is no hiding from the fact that is not both cowardly and grotesquely selfish. The suffering and injustice in this world today, which in truth is even greater than it was fifty or one hundred years ago, is appalling beyond what any words can describe. How can anyone look upon this with calm, banal indifference?

Anyone that is not offended and indignant, and positively outraged by the state of our world, is either in severe denial, which means severe self-deceit, or else is severely numbed, which means more dead than alive, and darkened and eclipsed, at least temporarily, of the heart and the mind.

Are we alive in heart and mind as well as body, or have we become the hollow men – and, if so, what are we going to do about it in order to reclaim and unearth our basic intelligence, our natural compassion and our common sense? These are the most critical questions facing us now, in this frankly bewildered age of late industrial civilization (sic).

Compassion requires vigour, as well as the courage of self-honesty – not timidity and meek docility, or excessive deference to what is considered "polite" avoidance of unpleasant realities, or even reserved speech about such atrocities or serious problems. When it began to dawn on more than a few human beings that slavery is an utter abomination and crime against human-ity, no meek words were sufficient to condemn the practice, or to end it. There is a time for the gentleness of a lamb, and there is a time for the ferocity of a lion. To be a lamb at heart and in general is wise as well as benign, beneficial and also intelligent. But to be all lamb at all times, is to be brain-dead and heart-numbed, as well as neutered and eviscerated – spineless, inert, opaque, and of little use to anyone. We have no time left for such absurdities.

What words other than 'dark satanic mills' could Blake have used to accurately and honestly describe the horrors of the early industrial revolution? How could he mince words then? How could Dickens? How could Mark Twain mince words in condemning American imperialism, Einstein in warning against nuclear war, Martin Luther King Jr. and Malcolm X in condemning racism and class-based injustice, or Rachel Carson in raising the alarm and warn-ing us all that we are destroying our environment? And how can we possibly mince words now, when humanity and the earth are being savagely pillaged and degraded? To do so would be, it seems to me, utterly repugnant, and thor-oughly revolting to every shred of decency in the human spirit. To be overly polite at such times would seem to me to spit upon the face of humanity and all that is good. I for one cannot do so. If that be rude, then call me a rude boy, and I accept the charge with pride, and will know that I am in good company.

What I am trying to convey is that the writing in the book has varying moods, and some of them may be pleasant like a spring breeze, or quiet, like a forest brook in the full warmth and fragrant richness of summer; while others hit like a full gale or even a hurricane, a bolt of lightning, a bucket of cold water, or a mailed glove to the cheek in a slap of reality that shocks, and cuts through the delirium which haunts us in our malaise, despair, rationalizations and fog of denial. I can see no way around it. This is how it was written.

Chogyam Trungpa spoke of idiot compassion, which is the compulsion to be gentle at all times, even when firmness or strong words or actions are needed. I do not wish to fall into that, for that would be pointless and self-defeating. The general rule of gentleness is best. There is also a time for ferocity, a time for the overturning of tables, a time to draw one's sword and cut through all obstacles, shackles and chains, with a force that is sufficient to the task at hand. We are talking about the liberty and the well-being, and even the survival of billions of human beings and other living beings on this earth. We are not talking about cutting butter to spread upon toast. Something more firm and more direct and incisive than a tender stroke with a butter knife is needed now. If that frightens some, then take that as a warning: the conversation will not at all times be fawning and demure. The text is uplifting, inspiring and empowering, I would say, or certainly it aims to be, and ultimately, extremely hopeful – in fact, not hopeful, but utterly confident – but it is also ruthlessly and brutally frank.

I am firmly committed to the principle, and also the superior strategy, of non-violence, but I am not, and cannot in good conscience or even basic sanity, be opposed to a sometimes bold and fierce manner of speech. We have been lost in illusions for too long. Our illusions are too pretty, too comforting, too fastidiously drawn to our sides, too deeply held, and far, far, far too dangerous to us now, for these words to be anything but cutting, when cutting is what is needed to sever us from those fairy tales and delusions that now endanger all our lives, and our children's lives. No, if for no other reason, then for the simple reason of the defence of the children of this earth, and the defence of their future, the wording of this text is both frank and uncompromising, fierce and unflinching: things *must* change for the sake of our children, and no words will be minced here in their defence. In a word, cowardice is unacceptable – too many lives are at stake, and too many *young* lives at that.

For those who are too delicate, fragile or easily offended for such sobering reading, there are many other books out there, and they need not bother with this one. For those who brave on, I would hope that not too many get their knickers in a knot if the book is exactly as presented here: fierce, frank and uncompromising.

Those who want only pleasant reading will have to look for children's books. The adult world is not always pleasant. Moreover, to turn our faces away from the unpleasantries is to turn a blind eye and a cold shoulder to the suffering and the injustice in the world, and that is an act of moral cowardice and callousness which cannot be indulged, and will not. For those who prefer sedate, lukewarm and highly restrained discourse only, where all passion is stripped away and all facts and views are stated with the greatest of gentility and politeness, if not meek and fawning evasiveness and euphemisms, the obituaries may be more suitable. But these are not the obituaries. These are the odes to joy and to life, and a rallying of the human spirit to meet the call to defend and to secure our future and the future of all life on this earth. If that be too immodest or too far from staid for some, so be it. It is too late for niceties. Compassion does not mean always being nice. June and Ward Cleaver are not the saviours of the world, nor even sane role models. I wish to embolden the bold. I am less concerned about displeasing the timid – although their assistance would be greatly appreciated.

In the spirit of the Socratic tradition, let it be said that a good question is better than a poor answer: so let us question, and question all – the answers will come in their own time: rushing them, or worse, assuming them, leads only to a perpetuation of ignorance and delusion. Nothing but presumption will be seen if we mistake our assumed knowledge for truth, and refuse to question the unquestionable assumptions of our day. Take no one's word on anything: let us see for ourselves. No certainty is unquestionable. Let that be rule one.

I must say, I sometimes think of this writing as having, on occasion, the bearing of an axe-wielding Viking raider compared with that church mouse who called himself Zarathustra and spoke of philosophy with a hammer. This, I am afraid, is philosophy with a broad sword and sledge hammer.

Only illusion is threatened. None who value truth should fear it, but instead welcome it. The truth is liberation; illusion, nothing more than fairy tales – what, therefore, is there to fear?

You do not defend the truth with a feather-duster. Nor do you speak in defence of human beings and life on earth with a timid or apologetic air. It is time to smash the clay feet. Get your warrior on. It is needed. If humanity is to survive, we will have to be bold. And there is no question as to "if" – therefore, the response that is required is abundantly clear.

"Because you are neither hot nor cold, but only luke-warm,
I spit you out of my mouth."

– St. John of Patmos

"Evil flourishes only when good men do nothing."

– Anonymous

"If you are afraid of writing anything that might offend someone,
why write anything at all?"

– Thomas Merton

SOME LIKE BACH'S AIR Suite, some like Tchaikovsky's 1812 Overture. I love them both, and find they suit specific times. For everything there is a season. If dry, monolithic, sombre uniformity is the preference of some, then this text may dismay; but if variety is the spice of life, and passion in the realm of ideas does not offend, then it may kindle the spirit and enliven the blood, as well as the mind.

I guess then I have talked myself into doing what I am certain I would have done anyway, thinking aloud here with you this day, for I could in truth do no other: life is precious, human beings and all living beings are precious, and things need to change now, in order for life to go on, on this beautiful little planet we call home. The book rests as it is. I hope it will be of some help. I cannot tell you how deeply that feeling is in me.

I realize that the Western academic tradition has become one in which dispassion and the pretence of neutrality and objectivity are worshipped and revered as axioms of our present scholastic times – and I do mean scholastic – just as it has been the tradition to speak in the third person, as if the author were a disembodied intellect, floating with god-like powers of vision above all the mundane world and lesser beings of mere mortals; and while I can see some benefit to this mode of writing and discourse, it is not mine, and moreover, it is not always the best mode to pretend to neutrality, nor to be dispassionate, arid, obtuse and functionally banal, able to rouse only the most bookish to liveliness, and then only to bookish study or talk, and not to action, more often than not.

Just as we should not pretend to omniscience, we should not pretend to neutrality, for both are deceitful. Moreover, nor can we afford, morally or practically, to be dispassionate when it comes to issues affecting the well-being of others. As Einstein and Howard Zinn both said, you can't be neutral on a moving train: and to be mousey or placid in the face of evil, is evil itself, or at least complicity with it – certainly it is ineffectual, and it is cowardly.

There is a time and place for most everything, and now is a time for the cutting through of illusions with all the ferocity that is required to accomplish the task – and nothing less. Our survival hangs upon it. We cannot be overly reserved now. Shelve the tweed smoking jacket and bring out the black leather, metaphorically speaking – or the chain mail. (If we cannot inject a little lightness and humour amidst our very serious discussions, by the way, we are likely dead in our tracks.) To the more staid of the academy I would urge: get off the fence and into the street – the revolution is now. And if I am wrong and it is not, it won't matter anyway, for we are all finished. It is truly now or never. We have run out of time. It cannot be stressed enough. What gadfly does it take to rouse academia from its slumber? I do not know, but we need such a one now, and without delay. Socrates come quick, and never mind the hemlock, for the children and the elders alike are mad with malaise. We need you.

It is action as well as reflection that is required of us now, and action requires, at times, something more rousing than a soliloquy to boredom. 'Yes, we're rallying people to go off and defeat the Nazis and fascism, and we're.... yawn.... very.... snore... earnest about it....' Right.... Imagine if Churchill had spoken like most academics write, with all the fire and the power of a neutered, tethered mule: we'd all be wearing jack boots and singing the praises of the Fuhrer – or else be either dead or in prison camps. Can the point be made more clearly? We need to rouse people to action, not put them to sleep. Put away the chloroform, and get out the Zen stick and the soap box. If you believe in what you are saying, and it is not a trivial subject, then say it with passion – or at least in a lively and perhaps compelling way. Yes, there are times for rousing speeches.

Reflection, too, often requires words that cut through our baggage of assumed truths, that can cut open the opaque plastic bubble which is now asphyxiating our minds, our lives and our hearts – otherwise reflection is simply an intellectual parlour game with no real results in terms of our underlying psychology or deepest presumptions: everything remains on the surface, and nothing substantially changes, for it is all a matter of intellect and theory, not lived experience or visceral understanding. Passion and power are needed in our discourse now, or we will remain in our mental and social ruts, until we are buried under the weight of our own inertia, and our species is no more.

To hell with our social and literary and intellectual conventions – at least when and where they have become obstacles to real progress or awareness. Throw them out, or push them aside. We cannot afford to be overly sentimental now, nor overly fastidious with regards to custom or mere outward form. We must see, and we must act. These two priorities are vital now, and all else is dispensable: a nicety at best, to be worked with or around; or an obstacle at worst, to be moved to the side – forcefully if necessary.

What matters more: our survival, or our conventions? Do we really have to think about that question? Our conventions can be forfeited, and without hesitation – especially when they impede our basic common sense and natural compassion. Etiquette and convention must always come after and below compassion, or we have truly lost our minds, along with our common sense.

Literary and academic conventions are no exception. The hallowed is life, not reflections of life, not theories about life, *and not* the ivory tower's pretences or protocols. Compassion is the overarching value, not form – and hence, effective action and communication are what matter, and not whether we have indexed and cross-referenced our semicolons or portrayed a sufficiently stuffy indifference to life. And academia needs to be shaken up as much as any other area of society, we must mention while we are on the subject. Pretence and posturing must give way to substance – and they will, we can assure you. Let the rebels rise and speak. The orthodoxy has failed us.

But this is painting an overly rosy picture of academia. Academics have traditionally lined up to defend the ruling powers and the status quo, and any line of orthodoxy that supports these same tends to be in fashion. Only the few and the brave have dared to challenge the reigning orthodoxy or the ruling powers, for the simple reason that academia is a hierarchical power structure, and as a hierarchical institution of social power, it tends to reproduce itself, as all institutions and particularly all hierarchical institutions tend to do, such that those who rise up are those who serve the established powers, and those who replicate the 'known truths' and universally accepted wisdom. The few rebels and iconoclasts and free thinkers are the true leaders. The rest are sheep and collaborators, or as Howard Zinn put it, the guardians of the establishment.

Not only is academia banal and indifferent, fence-sitting or complacent, far too often and too habitually when it comes to issues of significance, but even worse, it is on the side of injustice and stupidity more often than not. The unspoken and underlying motto seems to be career before conscience – and heaven help anyone who dares defy that maxim. There is a long way to go to liberate academia from medieval scholasticism and subservience to empire. This is a call to action, and a shout to defy the norm of passive acquiescence, blind servility, devout servitude, abject apologetics of power, and mediocre mouthing of dry opinions without passion or soul. There are many great minds among the ivory towers of Babylon, and many that could be great, should they ever lose their excessive deference to authority. May we hear more from them, and may the norm of dispassionate doldrums, and fearful, cowardly 'neutrality' fade from sight. Let us see a little more spine and fire in that realm which is supposed to be a realm of thought – a little more moral and intellectual courage, and a lot less unthinking and timid conformity and obedience to power.

It might be clear from this that I don't write for everyone. I write for the benefit of everyone, but not with everyone in mind as an audience. I don't write for morons – meaning, I'm not trying to speak to those who are in love with their ideology to such an extent that no rational thought or meaningful discussion is possible.

Morons, by the way, are simply people who make too many assumptions. There is no other way to be a moron. And the greatest of morons are those with the most rigid, self-sanctified and unquestionable assumptions. To avoid being a moron, we should question every assumption. This is the simple and very effective antidote and recipe for maintaining or regaining our basic sanity and natural intelligence. The path to basic clarity is the clearing away of all the veils of illusion. It is the path of un-learning. Often, our education and assumed "knowledge" is the barrier. And more often than not, in fact, our higher education is really a form of higher indoctrination. As the Paul Simon song goes, "When I look back at all the crap I learned in high school, it's a wonder I can think at all. But my lack of education never harmed me none – I can see the writing on the wall."

I don't write for people who have circled the wagons and have decided in advance that they and their club are the only ones who know anything, and are solely and completely in the right. I also do not write for those who are pathologically greedy; for those who are callous beyond all present attempts at communication; or those who are megalomaniacal in their pursuit of power and self-aggrandizement; and I don't write for Sophists and intellectual courtesans who will argue for any position, or adopt any position, so long as it pays well.

> *But then they send me away to teach me how to be sensible,*
> *logical, responsible, practical*
> *And they showed me a world where I could be so dependable,*
> *clinical, intellectual, cynical...*
> *I said now, watch what you say, or we'll be calling you a radical,*
> *a liberal, fanatical, criminal*
> *Won't you sign up your name, we'd like to feel you're acceptable,*
> *respectable, presentable, a vegetable*
>
> *– The Logical Song*

I am speaking as a fellow human being, and one with imperfect knowledge and many faults, to those men and women who have a basic sanity remaining which they have not yet lost touch with – meaning, their natural intelligence is still intact, along with their natural compassion and concern for others, and they are still able to both think and feel, and to examine things in a more or less honest and reflective, thoughtful manner. That is, I am writing for the great majority; and not the lost ideologues, the cold, the hardened hearts, nor for pathologically egocentric minds. The latter group tend to be in positions of power, or service to power – as this is the age of empires, and empire is antithetical to both sanity and compassion, and to serve or be devoted to empire requires the self-chosen, unconscious eclipsing of our innate compassion and common sense. But that is something that is changing, as the entire social order is changing, and rapidly; and the age of empires, including this latest empire of global neo-feudal corporatism, is crumbling and passing away, though most see it not.

> *"Pain is the breaking of the shell of your awareness."*
>
> *– Khalil Gibran*

> *"I fear no truth, and fear no falsehood."*
>
> *– Thomas Jefferson*

What matters? Love and knowledge. Or to be more precise, compassion and wisdom. Pursuing these, living by these to every extent of our present ability, makes our lives rich, and makes our lives meaningful. To keep these two beacons in mind or in heart will steer us ever on toward our highest destiny, which is the realization of our true nature – which is far greater than we tend to imagine or dare to dream. There are those with a jaundiced, cynical or dark view of life or human nature. They will be pleasantly surprised, in the end. We are faulted, but our greatest treasures have yet to be shared, or even discovered. Bring out your best. The world needs it now, and we all deserve to enjoy the treasures that lie within.

Cooking is 10% theory or instruction, and 90% experimentation. Life? The same. So we have made errors. The important thing is that we do not repeat the same mistakes over and over, ad nauseam or ad infinitum. Let us have remorse where we have made mistakes, learn from everything and all experiences, and move on. This moment and this day are completely new.

Bless you, all. And I hope you enjoy the read. More importantly, I hope it is in some small way, or perhaps in larger ways, liberating, illuminating, inspiring or empowering, or all of the above. That may sound like a high aim, but that was the objective. I humbly pray that there was some success in this.

I truly and fully agree with one of my greatest heroes, Henry David Thoreau, when he said, "Ultimately men hit only what they aim for... therefore, they had better aim high." What would be the point of aiming for anything less? We are too noble of nature, and too great in our potentials, for anything less than this. The values and the ideals of the Renaissance and Enlightenment are worth pursuing, and are not yet nearly as fully realized as we fool ourselves into believing – nor as they can be, and *will be*.

May we sever all chains, cut through all illusions, and find the freedom within and without to make this life and this world the beautiful, and also just and peaceful place, it still yet can be. May we find the courage within us, the inspiration, the fortitude, and all the tenacity and deep commitment, and also the joy that fuels the fire, to accomplish these aims – and not only for our own benefit, but for the benefit of every living being in this small, glorious world we call home. Above all, we can and must, and, I believe, will do so, for the sake of our children, and all of the children of this earth. They deserve a future, and they deserve a beautiful, happy, just and free world in which to live. This is attainable, I promise you. This is my prayer. And this is my conviction. And this is my commitment to you: I will do all that is in my power to aid us in accomplishing these goals.

The only true enemy is illusion, and it has always been so. Today, the major forces blocking progress towards a peaceful, just, free and democratic society are the illusions of *corporatism, nihilism and materialist reductionism*. And the primary obstacle to overcoming these three main barriers to a better world for all is the *pervasive illusion of powerlessness among the people*, and the resulting childish habit of excessive and undue deference to authority. As Thoreau said, we respect what is respected, not what is respectable, and hence, behave as wooden men, as hollow men. Find me a true man or true woman in this desolation, and I will show you the future. Underlying these four illusions is a fundamental *dichotomy of the mind*, which is itself an illusion, and which is the root of all illusion, as well as all suffering and evil. This deepest illusion must be unearthed, exposed to the light of day, rigorously analyzed and examined, and thoroughly destroyed, by thoroughly seeing through it. We do not lack in technology or in knowledge, in skill or in tools, or in money, capital or resources that are needed to make a better world – we lack in will, and we lack in will because we are presently mired and entangled in illusion, in a thick and heavy haze that clouds the mind.

These five illusions are what hold us back and bog us down, more than anything else at this time. These five illusions must be crushed using every means available. That is precisely what this text sets out to do. May our illusions die swiftly and peacefully, may the death of illusion be met with celebration and joy, not timidity and fear, or a feeble clutching at our blinders and chains, and may humanity live in well-being, freedom, justice and peace. May a new renaissance be born, and may all beings in this world have the greatest of happiness. This will be done. It is time.

JTR
November 18, 2011

"It is the breaking of the root vow to refuse to give correction
when correction is needed,
even if you cannot do it in the best possible way."

– The Bodhisattva Vows

"Anything good that I have been able to accomplish,
all credit goes to God.
I can take credit only for the errors."

– Malcolm X

"Everything I have written is chaff compared to what I have seen."

– Thomas Aquinas

"A single step on the path of enlightenment
is greater than being the ruler of the entire universe."

– The Buddha

"Do not take anyone's word for things,
not even someone you respect, not even myself.
Examine things for yourself."

– The Buddha

"Sit down before a fact like a little child,
and be prepared to give up every preconceived notion…
or you shall learn nothing."

– T.H. Huxley

"Be yourself.
Everyone else is already taken."

– Oscar Wilde

❧

THE GLOBAL FINANCIAL COUP AND THE COMING REVOLUTION

The real story of the
2012 US Presidential election
– the story the mass media missed altogether –
and the critical lessons from history
that we must learn now

"Those who do not learn from history are doomed to repeat it."

– Anonymous

"Evil can flourish only when good people do nothing."

– Anonymous

"Repeating the same actions and expecting different results is the very
definition of insanity."

– Albert Einstein

A RECENT ARTICLE FROM THE *Huffington Post* splashes a headline that declares that the mass media completely missed the biggest story of the 2012 US presidential election. Then the usually banal and blindly partisan Huff-Post does its usual job, and goes on to completely obfuscate the matter entirely. The article not only completely misses the point, not only further distracts the people from the real issue, the central issue, but gives yet another gloss of the 2012 election. But the important point is not the sloppy and uncritical, virtually mindless "journalism" of the *Huffington Post*. The far bigger issue is the complete misrepresentation of the election and the entire state of politics in the US by a compliant and subjugated mass media broadly – both mainstream and "alternative." The bigger issue yet, the central issue, is the state of democracy in America, and the questions of a) where does real power lie? and b) what is to be done about it?

The biggest issue of the 2012 election – and overwhelmingly so – was that it was a total farce. The two candidates and the two parties share virtually identical policies on the major issues, both foreign and domestic. That is, 1) they both favour the interests of the business elite at the expense of the people and the earth – which is not surprising, because that's who funds their elections and gets them into office; 2) they both favour a domestic policy of a police state at home – Obama simply expanded and intensified Bush's war on democracy, civil liberties, human rights and freedom at home as well as abroad; 3) they both favour aggressive militarism and imperial warfare abroad – again, Obama expanded and intensified Bush's wars; 4) they are both in favour of austerity measures for the people, spending cuts to old age security, Medicare and Medicaid; 5) they are both in favour of tax cuts for the super-rich and the corporate elite – they just disagree on how big they should be; and 6) they both favour multi-trillion dollar "bailouts" for the too-rich-to-fail who rule the country and fund their "elections."

So the American people had fascist war monger A or fascist war monger B to choose from. That was the real story of the 2012 US presidential "election." The real story is that for the moment at least, democracy is dead in America.

Chomsky has rightly said that "Obama is the biggest human rights abuser in the US" – yet Obama is portrayed in the media as a progressive. This is madness. Some are simply being deceitful; some are being deceived. The fact is that Obama and Romney are the Tweedle Dee and Tweedle Dum of militarist, anti-democratic corporate rule.

"The assault on civil liberties under the Obama administration has been worse than under Bush...What we have undergone in this country is a

kind of coup d'état in slow motion – a corporate coup d'état, where all the impediments to corporate capitalism have been lifted, by both of the major political parties....And it is now incumbent upon all of us who care about those who suffer, to make the personal commitment which is required by civil disobedience to stand up against these forces."

– Chris Hedges, "Third World America"

The big story is that the American people are asleep, while their country is being pillaged and turned into a police state. That is the real story.

Fortunately, however, the people are beginning to awaken. That's why approximately half of Americans voted "No confidence" – and didn't vote. Obama won with a "sweeping victory" we are told – ya, he got a sweeping victory with approximately 29% of the American people voting for him. In any other country, we'd call this election a sham if we saw figures like that. But not in the good ol' USA. Here it's proclaimed as a stunning populist victory. It's a joke – a very bad joke.

Roughly 20% of the people voted for Romney, and 29% for Obama. Roughly 51% didn't vote, and most of them refused to vote because they rightly viewed the election as a choice between two candidates who both work for the same ruling corporate elite who fund their elections and put them in power, demanding favours and preferential treatment in return.

It's time to put the sham aside, and call it like it is: America has become a fascist nation, where the business elite have merged with the state. As Mussolini himself defined it, that is fascism, and that's what America has now. Obama has sided with the elite fraction of a percent on every major issue, and at the expense of the people, democracy, constitutional rule and the environment.

It's time we speak the truth, and stop telling ourselves lies. It's time to face the facts. Democracy in America has been hijacked by the corporate elite, who have thrown the people and the constitution overboard. That is the real story. Now, it is time for democratic revolution. Let's get on with it, and stop pretending we're living in some other reality.

The Obamaphiles are going to have to come back to earth some time. Reality will force them to, sooner or later. It's shocking that it hasn't yet with even more people, but it will definitely happen to the rest. The gloves are coming off, and the mask is about to slip. A class war is being waged by the 0.1% on the other 99.9% – and the class warfare is just getting into high gear. We haven't seen anything yet – compared to what is unfolding now, and what is coming.

Obama isn't the messiah. He isn't even a democrat. He's a member of the Democratic Party of course, but he is no democrat. Let's try to deal with reality here. He is a corporatist – he believes in the merger of business and the state – and we can ask Mussolini what that means. Moreover, Obama is working for someone – and it is not the American people.

Where does real power lie in the world today? The United States continues to dominate the world economically and militarily, and through this lever-age, also diplomatically, through sabotaging international agreements – for example, blocking international agreements which seek to create serious action on climate change.

The US empire is in obvious and rapid decline, and is crumbling, although it is still very powerful, and extremely dangerous. But real power does not lie with the elected "democratic" government of the United States in Washington. Real power does not lie with the White House or Congress. Real power resides, as it has since the National Security Act was passed in 1947, with the National Security Council, the Pentagon, and the intelligence community which dominates and controls both of these powers, as Gore Vidal, Bill Moyers and others have pointed out.

Taking the analysis further and deeper, it is clear that in turn these forces are controlled by the business elite of the country, and in particular, by Wall Street, by the financial elite. But Wall Street itself is just a junior partner in the new global empire of trans-national corporate rule. Wall Street and the entire corporatist empire are controlled by old money from Europe, as they have been for a very long time.

The US empire has now been completely swallowed by the larger, more powerful, and now globally dominant trans-national corporate empire. The bankers have taken over the world. The Pentagon, the CIA and the elected US "government" – the politicians who work as vassals and servants to the international financial masters – are most definitely real powers in the world today, of course. But these powers of the waning US empire are now simply the bought and paid for, hired thugs of the global financial elite. The game has changed. We now live in a different world.

What we are looking at is rule by a neo-feudal band of corporate and financial oligarchs that have no real allegiance or loyalty to any nation, or to the people of the earth. What is to be done in response? Certainly the response needs to be far more thoughtful and far more bold than continuing to pretend that federal elections in the United States mean anything. Local and state elections may still be relevant, and are, and much can be accomplished there. But at the federal level, elections are a distraction and a waste of time.

The two parties of the business elite continue to rule, no matter who wins. In such a situation, where the democratic process has been taken over by a small band of elites, and the democratic system is no longer functioning – other than as a charade, a mechanism for lulling the people to sleep, or keeping them distracted, docile and bemused, and a system which continues to perpetuate the anti-democratic rule of a handful of international bankers and financial elites – elections and petitions are utterly insufficient to the task, and are in fact a blood-letting: they drain away the vitality of the people which could otherwise be used for real social change, and for winning their democracy back.

In such a situation where the electoral and democratic process has been hijacked by the richest few who have seized power and rendered democracy effectively null and void, and where, furthermore, rule by the elite is leading to the destruction of life on earth and the end to human beings on this planet, the only two remaining responses are revolution or death. One would hope the more intelligent choice would be made.

There is no greater master of the art of strategy than Sun Tzu, the author of the Chinese classic, *The Art of War*. What is not widely known is that Sun Tzu's manual is not just about war, but about peace. His first principle is that war has a horrific cost to nations, communities and human lives, and therefore, peace should be sown and sought, harmony maintained, and war avoided at all costs. What is also not widely known is that there is no better textbook on the art of strategy that has ever been written. And if we are interested in success, then we must also be interested in strategy: for if we know nothing of strategy, then we will not likely succeed – in fact, without intelligent strategy, we will almost certainly fail.

Sun Tzu shows us how we can succeed – even against what appear on the surface to be overwhelming odds. And one element of which he speaks, one element in the art of strategy and attaining victory, is becoming increasingly relevant today, in light of the accelerating global ecological crisis.

Sun Tzu speaks of what he calls "death ground." He said that to ensure victory, place your men where they cannot retreat, and they will be victorious against all odds. When individuals know there is no option of retreat, and that the only options are to fight or die, they will draw forth tremendous strength from within. We saw Sun Tzu's principle of death ground on the beaches of Normandy. There was no option of retreat. The ocean was behind the allies when they landed on the beaches. Men were loaded with gear and could not possibly swim back to England. Because they could not retreat, but were on death ground, they fought with uncommon courage, and were victorious in what seemed like an utterly hopeless situation. That battle on the beaches of Normandy was decisive of course, and the Nazis were defeated precisely because the allies stood on death ground, and were forced to fight or die.

In may be appalling to think about, and it is certainly horrible, but it is a fact, nonetheless: at the beginning of the 21st century, all of human kind is now standing on death ground. The basis of life on earth is rapidly being destroyed. Scientists and even the World Bank say that we will be extinct in as little as fifty years or possibly less if we do not make major changes now. And yet, it is the reigning corporate and financial elite, who have taken over both the global economy and the political process, and who have hijacked democracy, who are now the major obstacles to the very changes we most urgently need. The long and short of it is this: we either have a second wave of democratic revolutions, and remove the corporate and financial elite from power, or we die, and humanity will be no more.

As the awareness of this new reality begins to sink in, and the people awaken to the gravity of the danger and the urgency of action, it will become clear to all that we are on death ground, environmentally speaking, and often in other ways: and we must fight or die.

Many baby boomers and people who are older, and many young people as well, remain complacent, despite the growing and obvious dangers, thinking, presumably, that they won't live long enough to witness the extinction of humanity, so the environmental crisis won't affect them. This is not only grossly unethical towards the nearly half of the world's population who are children, but it is also extremely short-sighted. Unless we are stupid enough to launch World War III and destroy the planet with a bang, if we are foolish enough to allow the corporate and financial elite to continue to effectively rule over the world, and are not wise enough to make a stand now, we will go out with a whimper. And as we continue to sow destruction on the earth, we will increasingly move into a very dark time, where life is not worth living – far before we actually become extinct. So the question is not only democratic revolution or death, it is worse: democratic revolution, or slow death by self-asphyxiation and poisoning, through a short-lived but very ugly dark age.

It makes sense to stand now, clearly. Anything else is mindless, as well as obscenely unethical, disgraceful and cowardly – and anything else means a slow and painful self-destruction.

Democratic revolution is now urgently needed. And it is going to happen, mark my words. The people are waking up, and the people are fed up. The writing is on the wall.

It is time for real change.

The Normandy invasion teaches us another critical lesson. When the Allies landed on the beaches of Normandy on DDay, and successfully fought their way against overwhelming odds, pushing back the Nazi forces, another element became decisive as well. The Nazis needed reinforcements to hold back and defeat the Allied forces, but Hitler kept a strict command and control structure, and no major troop deployments could be conducted without his direct approval. Hitler had also given strict instructions that he was not to be disturbed while he was sleeping. At a critical moment, when the Nazis desperately needed reinforcements sent in, it happened that Hitler was sleeping. But reinforcements could not be sent, because Hitler did not approve them. The result was the turning point in the war, and the ultimate defeat of the Nazis. The Nazis were defeated precisely because they had over-centralized power.

Had Hitler not centralized power so excessively, had power been more decentralized, the Nazis would have been far more powerful, and far harder to defeat. But of course, the central idea of fascism is to centralize all power in the hands of the few. It is for this reason that fascism will always be defeated, sooner or later.

When power is over-centralized, the head can be cut off, or as in the case of the Normandy invasion, the communication between the head and the body can be disrupted. In either event, the over-centralization of power leads to the collapse of that power, as Normandy and the defeat of fascism shows.

Over-centralization of power leads to a rigid inflexibility, as well as a diminished pool of minds and creativity that are drawn upon, and both of these factors lead to weakness and instability. As the Taoist teachings say, soft overcomes hard: what is fluid and flexible can bend, shift, adapt, maneuver, and triumph over what is rigid, hard and inflexible. And overly centralized powers are always monolithic, rigid and inflexible, and therefore doomed to self-destruction and collapse.

Great concentrations of centralized power may look impressive, but they are castles made of sand. And the people are the sea. The tide of history always erodes the foundations of such sand castles, until finally they collapse, and are washed away.

Coordination and unity are essential, but centralization of power is not. Decentralized power provides more adaptability, flexibility, manoeuvrability and resiliency, and is therefore stronger. For this reason, among others, the people are always more powerful than any empire or centralized power in society. The people should take this lesson to heart, and act with courage, confidence and boldness. They will triumph.

What is happening in the world today is an extreme over-centralization of power, as Catherine Austin Fitts and others have said, and as Orwell and Huxley foresaw decades ago. The trend is obvious and unmistakable. Excessive centralization of power has taken place within the US, and in virtually every country world-wide, with few exceptions, by way of a financial coup: and power is being centralized globally as well, and at increasing speed, in the hands of a few ruling global financial elites. Such over-centralization of power is not only antithetical to democracy, and completely at odds with both freedom and democracy, leading to a show-down between democracy and elite rule, but over-centralization also and invariably leads to greater instability. It is like building a house of cards: the higher the tower of cards, the more unstable it becomes, until finally, it collapses.

The financial elite are busy building a ziggurat. It is the tower of Babel. And the higher the tower, the more unstable it is. The greater the centralization of power, the more assured it is of collapse. With power in the world now extremely concentrated and centralized globally, this newest of empires is anything but stable. In fact, it is ready to collapse.

We should not be overly impressed by the staggering concentration of power in the world today, or the centralization of power globally in the hands of a few bankers and financial elites. It is exactly this over-centralization of power that guarantees the house of cards will fall, and this latest of empires will crumble.

The people will be victorious, for the excessive centralization of power is doomed to failure. The people always hold the greater power, even though their power is spread out among the grassroots – and precisely because their power is diffuse, decentralized, and without a single centre. The people will triumph in the end. And the turning point is upon us now.

Sun Tzu, the unrivalled master of the art of strategy says, "To win one hundred battles is not impressive. To win without fighting is." Gandhi and Martin Luther King Jr. would agree – and for moral as well as strategic reasons.

The people and the earth are being defeated, and they are being defeated, generally speaking, without fighting. They are being defeated, in general, not by ordinary weapons, but by what Max Keiser calls "financial weapons of mass destruction." They are being defeated by a global financial coup.

What is needed now is a Gandhi-style revolution. But for that to happen, first the people must embrace their power – and they do not embrace their power by continuing to yield it up to the powerful, which they persist in doing at present.

Sun Tzu also said that it is more important to out-think your enemy than to fight him. This bodes well for the people, since the ruling elite have the overwhelming advantage when it comes to raw force or physical power – military force, paramilitary and security forces, control over the mass media and the cultural power which that yields, and also financial and economic power. But superior force does not ensure victory. Vietnam proved that beyond all shadow of a doubt. The world's leading superpower, with incomparably greater military and economic power than any empire in the history of the earth, was defeated by a tiny population, with almost no military or economic power by comparison. The defeat showed not only the victory of *strategy* over raw *power*, but the victory of the *mind* over the brute forces of *guns, bombs and money.*

This is what Gandhi called "soul force" – and it also enabled an impoverished and demoralized people, with virtually no weapons and no money, to break the back of what was at that time, the largest and most powerful empire in history, the British empire, and to claim and win freedom and democracy for the people of India.

It can be done. It has been done before. And it will be done again.

Only those who are ignorant of history believe they are powerless. History shows beyond any doubt or question, that when the people embrace their power and unite, they are successful, and they are victorious – no matter what the opposition may be, or how great it may seem.

All empires fall, sooner or later, and this latest empire, the empire of global finance, will fall as well – and democracy will be reborn when it does. And we don't have to wait for it, or convince the emperors to change their minds. Both responses would be foolish, and would lead to the destruction of humanity, as the earth is ravaged and destroyed, and human life is extinguished from the planet. What is needed is decisive action, and now.

When the people begin to use their common sense, and cease to shun it, as they do now, they will win, and they will reclaim their democracy from the financial and corporate elite who have stolen it. And in order to reclaim their common sense, they must also reclaim their dignity, and their power.

When the people begin to awaken to their power, and to embrace their power, they will be victorious, and they will reclaim their democracy, their world, and their future. Fortunately, that is exactly what is beginning to happen now.

JTR
December 12, 2012

BETWEEN TWO AGES:
A FORK IN THE ROAD, AND THE WRITING OF OUR FUTURE HISTORY

W̲E̲ L̲I̲V̲E̲ I̲N̲ M̲O̲M̲E̲N̲T̲O̲U̲S̲ times. We live in a time when the world is being reformed. I am, of course, not speaking about the physical world, although that is changing too, but the political, economic, social and cultural world in which we live – the world of human society. Never before have we seen such sweeping changes in human history, or such changes of profound consequence and import. But the changes are not yet fully defined, and the door to history written as we walk it, is still open. We still write our history as we go, and the future is yet ours to create. What will come next will be up to us. Right now, we live in between two ages. One age is dying. Another is not yet fully born. And moreover, there are two very different versions of our future that are being written now, as we speak, and two very different possible future worlds are sitting on the horizon before us. The differences between these two possible futures could not be more stark. Hence, we had better know what they are, and which we would like to see arise, and which avoided.

We live now, with an age that is passing into the memory of history; that is passing away. And we stand, while the present age is still dying, with a new era not yet fully emerged or defined, or even fully chosen. Two futures are being created in this present moment, and by two very different sets of people. We stand with our feet in the present, our present age fading into the past, and on the horizon before us, a clear fork in the road, and two very different future worlds laying before us down these two diverging paths.

It is now that we choose our future world. The bifurcation point is here: this is the moment of choosing. If we linger here in indecision, we will be pushed into one path, and our course will be set, and our path chosen for us. If we move with the drifting inertia of the time, then our course will be chosen by default, and the outcome will be regretted in the most profound and agonizing way. Only if we brace ourselves for reality, and face the full weight of our responsibility to future generations, to one another and to ourselves, then will we stand in wakefulness, and we will choose our future consciously – and that future alone, based on conscious choice by the people, and not on drifting malaise, indecision or passivity, will bring us a future worth having.

There are always in-between times, times between one period and another. We lost our job, or have quit our job for whatever reason, and are looking for another. We have decided our present career path is inadequate to our heart's calling, or to our pocketbook or our family responsibilities, or simply no longer what we want, and yet we have not yet found what our new career path will be. We have lost one thing, one time, one period or one way of life, and have not yet found the next. We are in a state of searching, or reflection – or grieving, or hoping, or apprehension, or excitement – or waiting, or creating, or building something new: but in all cases, we are between one period of our life, and another.

Between Rockefeller's monopolization of the world's new energy source, oil – which the world was soon to run on and become dependent upon, like a crack addict to his fix – and the emergence of the United States as the richest country in the world, there was a period in between. Between the Great Depression and the Keynesian New Deal, there was an in-between. Between the decimation of the European powers in World War II and the path chosen by the newly emerging two global super-powers of the U.S. and U.S.S.R., which was to shape the world for the next half century, there was a period in between.

Between the U.S. post-war decline and the unilateral abandonment of the gold standard and the beginning of the collapse or demolition of capital controls and the Bretton Woods system, which marked the birth of corporate globalization, was a period in between. Between the rise of the era of globalization in the early 1970's and the full emergence of a trans-national corporatocracy which came to effectively rule over virtually all nations, was a period in between, a period where many different paths could have been taken, and different paths could have been chosen.

Between 1970 and 2012, we, the people, the human beings of this earth, allowed the further consolidation of trans-national, global corporate powers, which have no allegiance to any nation or to democracy, to the people or to the earth – and in return, we gained exactly what we could have expected: the further erosion and undermining of democracy, the weakening and dissolution of the sovereignty of nations, the further acceleration of accumulation and concentration of real power, and along with it, great wealth, in the hands of the few and at the expense and loss of the many, and the rapid slide – or conscious, intentional drive, on the part of some – into a third-worldized, two-tiered society, where the richest few rule over the rest, while accumulating ever more wealth and power, and while the overwhelming majority slide further towards or deeper into poverty and despair, while their power is ever further wrested from them.

We now face a time where a decisive break from the past becomes not only possible, but inevitable. This is not the inevitability of something written beforehand. This is an inevitability written by our own hands. We have put in motion two distinct and divergent sets of patterns. There will be a struggle between these two possible futures. And we are now at the juncture, the breaking point, the point, as they call it in physics, of the bifurcation of potentialities. What we do or do not do now will be decisive for humanity and for all life on earth.

When I say a major transformation is now inevitable due to our actions and our neglect, I mean that the world is about to be transformed – and it will be transformed in one of two very different ways, depending on what we choose, or whether we choose not to choose, and so choose by default, by ceding our own power. In either case, the world as we know it is about to end: a new world will replace the familiar and the known – either for better or for worse. Which of the two possible worlds will replace the world we currently live in will be up to us. Currently, at least, there is no third option. Those who persist in the illusion that there is are in for a rude surprise.

We have been watching, if we have been watching, the nation-states of the world decline in power, while trans-national power blocks, such as the European Union or the NAFTA block of "Fortress North America," emerge as newly dominant global powers, taking over many powers from the weakening nation-states and effectively over-riding and eviscerating both sovereignty and democracy. The world is now more shaped by corporations than by nations, and nations are now more shaped by the global corporate rulers than by their own democratic processes.

We have slid from the era of nations and the nation-state, which is only a few hundred years old, into an era of trans-national powers and globalization. Along with the decline in relative power of the nation-state, we have seen the rapid decline and eclipse of the young democracies which so many of them represent. Remember that modern democracy is only two hundred some years old, so essentially all of them are new.

Some among the currently dominant elite are openly saying that the experiment in democracy and freedom is over. Others never wanted it in the first place. Whatever our view may be, there is certainly a major change that is underway, and the direction is abundantly clear: nation-states are being dissolved into trans-national bodies, and national democracy is being dissolved by the newly dominant global corporate powers. Whether we see this as a brave new world of wonderful, almost utopian dreams, or we see it as a descent into a nightmare realm of dystopian extremes, we had better pay attention, and also, realize that the point of juncture is now. We can still yet choose.

The only people who do not value freedom – at least for themselves if not for all human beings – are those who do not realize what they have, or what freedom means. The only people who do not value democracy, apart from the ruthlessly self-interested who wish to demolish it, are those who do not understand the alternative. Freedom and democracy are the only hope for a decent society and a decent life for all. If we do not understand the present fork in the road and the choices at hand, we will make very bad choices, and in all likelihood, will choose by default, by passively acquiescing as the choices are made for us. The result of such apathy will be disastrous, if that is what we decide to embody now. If we do not understand the value of freedom and democracy, we had better reflect on these now. They are being eroded, and are under attack. If we allow them to slip away, I assure you, we will deeply regret our indifference.

As was said, there are two distinct paths ahead, and two very different worlds or futures for humanity. One path ahead, is that led by a loose constellation corporatists, also known as globalists or neoliberals, neoconservatives, or simply and frankly put, anti-democratic, self-justifying and self-serving courtesans to empire, and most centrally, by the global financial and corporate elite. That path is a clear continuation of what we have been seeing for the past forty years: the further dissolution and elimination of the powers and sovereignty of the nation-states into trans-national entities; the further evisceration and dissolution of democracy; and the further transfer of real power, and with it, ever greater wealth, to the already globally dominant financial and business elite. This path is thoroughly anti-democratic, and represents the end of both freedom and democracy, as well as the further impoverishment of the vast majority of human beings and the further destruction of the earth, for the greater glory, wealth and power of the ruling elite. This is the path we are being led down by the currently reigning business elite, and the political and media elite who serve them. This future is being written as we speak, and it will be our future, if we do not decide consciously, and now, to choose otherwise, and to take a different path.

The other path is the path of empowerment of the people. It is the path of democracy. It is the path of freedom. It is the path of justice. It is the path of hope – of true hope. It is the path of the transformation of human society – not from a state of fledgling young democracies into a global corporate tyranny of neo-feudalism, but from a present tyranny of global corporate rule, into the birth of a truer, stronger, deeper and more vibrant democracy, which has benefits for all, and which will begin to renew this world, and heal its wounds. The path is clear for those with heart. And the choice ahead – the choice at hand, which can no longer be put off – could not be more clear.

A global awakening of humanity is occurring, and this path – the path of democracy, of empowerment and true hope for humanity – is equally as possible as the darker path, the path of global corporate feudalism. But it will not arise on its own. If this is the path of our choosing – as it should be if we are at all sane, if we have not yet lost all our faculties of basic common sense, natural compassion or enlightened self-interest – then we must actively choose it now, and work to bring this emerging future into fruition and to reality. It is as yet, a possibility. So too is a dark and brutal era ahead. Which will ensue depends upon what we do – or fail to do – right now.

What would Thomas Jefferson, Thomas Paine or Benjamin Franklin urge? They would most definitely urge us to defend liberty and democracy, and to ensure that these precious bright lights, our greatest of gifts, next to our own common sense, do not perish, but shine ever more brightly. And they would urge us to revolution, if that is what is necessary to secure liberty, democracy and justice for all, as it surely by now is.

What would the philosophers of the Enlightenment or the greatest minds of the Renaissance urge us to do? They would urge us to embrace in action as well as conviction, the values of liberty, equality and solidarity, of human rights and dignity for all, and of democracy – either on the level of the nation, or closer yet to the grassroots and to the people; and they would urge us to stand with our fellow human beings, and to seek the unfolding of the greatest potential of all human beings, by overturning every form of ignorance, illusion or oppression.

What would Jesus do? (I know it is not considered politically correct to speak of spiritual themes in the same breath as political issues, but such conventions are nonsense, and I will ignore them.) He would urge us to care for, defend and protect all human beings, as if they were our own brother or sister, our closest of family – for in truth, they are; and He would most certainly overturn the tables of the money changers who now rule the world, and throw them to the street. Whether we are Christian, Jewish, a follower of Mohammed or the Buddha, or have some other faith or no religion at all, I believe that if we are sincere in our hearts – if we have not yet eclipsed our hearts into a dark despair, or a quiet self-centredness, or a self-defeating resignation – that, we would have to agree, and follow this most common-sense and good-hearted example.

What would the Buddha advise? He would most certainly urge us to embrace our natural compassion, and to live with compassion for all, and to protect all living beings, and all human beings, from any form of violence, injustice or harm. He would disregard or subvert any form of caste or feudal arrangements of society which enrich and empower some while disempowering, degrading and dehumanizing others. He would not passively accept nor advise us to accept any form of society or human relations, such as we have now, where the few grow ever more staggeringly wealthy while the great majority are driven down into poverty or despair. He would advise, and urge, that our natural compassion be active, and not simply professed in speech, or embodied in a passive and pious hand-wringing.

What would Moses or Mohammed urge us to do? They would urge us to pursue the path of justice and righteousness, to love our neighbour, to seek to protect and to uplift all human beings, and to tolerate no injustice and no oppression, no matter how cleverly disguised. To abide evil is evil. To remain indifferent when others are suffering, or when human beings are being exploited, oppressed or otherwise maltreated, is a form of evil in itself. We must rise above that narrow indifference, and become what we are, which is just and good by creation, a spark of the divine – and this will come about by defending all human beings from tyranny and injustice of any kind, including the present tyranny of a greed-driven, self-aggrandizing, self-deifying, extraordinarily arrogant oligarchy of the merchant elite.

Merchants can be just or unjust, righteous or unrighteous, but they cannot be permitted to rule the world – not, at least, if justice is to prevail. Certainly they cannot be permitted to enthrone themselves as the new pharaohs, at the expense of the enslavement and subjugation of human beings around the world, which is the path we are now on.

The corporate oligarchs have a twisted view of Plato's ideal of the three orders of society, ruled by the philosopher kings. The oligarchs fancy themselves as glorious philosopher kings and the rightful rulers of the world – a view that is as delusional as it is dangerous, and it is dangerous in the extreme, make no doubt.

The currently reigning empire of global plutocracy, or rule by the super-rich, is not taking us into a bright and golden era, but backwards, into the darkest times of our past. This cannot, must not, and will not be permitted. In the name of God, in the name of common human decency, in the name of common sense, this current thrust towards a new and darker feudal era than the world has ever seen, must and will be halted now. Justice will prevail, and we are called to do what we can in the service of the highest of our nature, for the benefit of all, and so that a better world will be born.

Most importantly, most essentially, what do our own conscience, compassion and common sense dictate? I would say that, if we are honest with ourselves, and honest with what we are now facing, they would undoubtedly, most assuredly, and most definitely compel us to act now, and stand now, in defence of all living beings and all human beings on earth, and in defence of freedom, democracy, justice and well-being for all: and that this, if we have the honesty to face it, requires the defeat of the currently reigning global empire of corporate plutocracy, the returning of power to the people, and the renewal of democracy – and now, without delay.

We will either see the continued conscious drift into "a more controlled society," and in fact, "a highly controlled society," and witness "the crisis of democracy" be resolved by the elimination of democracy – in which case, we will return to a dark age of feudalism, in technotronic and technocratic, Orwellian form; or we will see the birth of freedom in a fuller degree, and the emergence of democracy in a fuller form, in which case, we will see, not a dark age of global feudal relations, with misery, subjugation and slavery for all but the few, but a new renaissance that will dwarf the first.

Let us choose wisely. The future is at hand. And the choice is now.

JTR
March 6, 2012

In honour of my daughters, on their birthday: and for their future, their brother's future, and the future of all children on earth.

UNITY IN DIVERSITY:
THE COMMONALITY AND UNDERLYING
UNITY OF HUMANKIND

ALL MEN AND WOMEN are created equal. We are born equal in worth as well as in our fundamental nature, regardless of relatively superficial differences in temperament, talents, outward appearance or states of mind. Basic goodness is within all individuals, no matter how covered over with habits of delusion that mask that true nature. But while basic goodness is universal and underlies our surface habits of mind and being, our potential for confused or even terrible states of mind and behaviour is universal as well. The insanity of egotism, greed and hate are equal-opportunity diseases of the mind: some from every culture, nation and people, and from both genders, fall into these in every generation, and we must admit also that the best and the worst are both within each of us, at least as potentialities. What we bring forward and nourish and cause to grow, is entirely up to us. Our potentials are ultimately the same, and they are limitless: it is a matter what we make of them. Human beings are in truth equal in worth, although very diverse in their myriad talents, strengths, personalities, tastes and natural proclivities. To recognize our commonality, our underlying unity, and our equality, is very important at this time in particular, to say it in the mildest possible way.

What we all have in common is at least five things: the capacity for suffering or happiness; the desire to be happy and to be free from suffering; the capacity for ignorance, greed and hate; the capacity for a basic, natural clarity of mind to be revealed, along with an equally natural instinct towards compassion and mutual aid; and a basic goodness and also unity that underlies every momentary or even long-standing confusion or error, and despite all differences and appearances of separation and division. This is the truth of the human species. When we see these commonalities and common realities more clearly, then we will live in a great deal more peace and also joy.

To put it concisely, no man is an island. Despite our rich and marvellous diversity as human beings, and underlying the rich and wonderful diversity of life, there is an underlying unity of being. Even more than a common ancestry, a common heritage, and certain fundamental shared traits, there is something more. We not only share much in common, and not only are we, and all beings and things, interdependent, but there is a unity at the heart of being which underlies and transcends our comparatively superficial differences.

There is nothing flaky, flippant, fuzzy, overly sentimental or imprecise about this statement: it is the core truth of our being. Modern physics is coming to realize it; Einstein, Schrodinger, Bohm – many of our greatest physicists have asserted it. Thoreau, Emerson, Whitman, Blake and others have proclaimed it. It is the underlying message at the heart of the mystical depths of all the great world religions. Our greatest poets, scientists, philosophers and sages have all told us of this, and have reminded us of our intuition of this fact. This central truth, the truth of the unity of being, is in all likelihood the single most important thing we need to recognize and to remember now. Any hopes of peace or ecological harmony, social justice or well-being for humanity, rest to a great extent upon whether or not we can see and admit to this central-most fact of our existence: that all beings and things are richly distinct and unique, and at the same time, utterly interdependent, and underneath the surface of things, united and one.

What I am about to say I cannot emphasize enough. What is needed for human beings to survive through our present crises and time of greatest peril, and to live wisely and well in this world, are a few basic things above all: a recognition of the preciousness and *basic goodness* of life; a renewed *confidence*, dignity and self-trust; a recognition of the kinship and *interdependence* of all peoples, beings and things; and a remembering of the underlying *unity* of being of which we all are a part.

It is hard to imagine how we will transcend our quarrels and also overcome our despoiling and destruction of the planet we live on, until and unless we achieve these few simple elements of restored common sense. These elements of awareness are the foundations of an enlightened democracy, an enlightened society, and even, at this point, a viable society of any kind.

The following essays will explore this subject in more depth, but again, only briefly – but we will return to the topic in later reflections.

We are one family. Closer even than that. We must come to realize this now – for our own well-being and quality of life today, and for a happy future for all.

JTR
November 17, 2011

VISIONS FOR HUMANITY IN THE 21ST CENTURY AND BEYOND:
LONG-TERM, SHORT-TERM AND IMMEDIATE GOALS

"The future holds ominous portent, and signs of great hope. Which result ensues depends largely upon what we make of the opportunities."

– Noam Chomsky

B EFORE WE GET INTO any discussion about possible visions for a better future, or any future, we need to make sure that our feet are properly planted firmly on the ground. We should, therefore, quickly reiterate an overview of just what is going on and where we stand, in this early part of the 21st century. Humanity is in a state of shock, a protracted state of numbed paralysis, induced by ongoing unrelenting crises. It is contextualization as well as solidarity – the gaining of clarity as to what is going on, along with a joining together with others in common cause – which overcomes this state of numbness, paralysis, shock and disorientation. We must discuss and reflect upon the state of our world, in order that we may understand it better, and also, that we may more truly and fully live, and not merely drift along in what has become the "profoundly abnormal norm," as social psychologist Erich Fromm put it, of quiet and unacknowledged desperation. The state of frozen paralysis, numbness and shock is now lifting across humanity, and we need to further that process of awakening, now, before we destroy ourselves and all future for humanity.

In a nutshell, after just over 200 years of what is a very gestational and early form of democracy, the corporate elite have now fully taken over, after having been dominant for over two centuries, and are running us headlong into a dark age of neo-Dickensian technocratic feudalism, and also off a cliff of ecological self-annihilation. Global polls show the people are very well aware of this fact, and a profound, world-wide crisis of legitimacy grows daily for the ruling global elite, who are terrified of losing their power – and with good reason.

"These are the money-changers.
This is as old as history.
Look at the facts and look at the numbers."
"The money-changers have taken over. That's all this is about."
"Look for a real hot summer of discontent,
raging across Eastern Europe, Europe, and, that's right, you guessed it,
the United States."

– World's leading trend analyst, and refreshingly honest,
clear-headed man, Gerald Celente

The media pundits and politicians don't tend to mention these obvious truths, but then, you wouldn't expect them to, when they are the bought and paid for, hired servants of big business, and big business wants to maintain the charade, the veneer – however thin – the pretence of democracy, because that makes it easier to rule over a hopefully compliant and docile public. But the people know what's going on, and many intelligent, well-informed writers, activists and commentators, outside the mainstream press, have spoken about the obvious facts.

As Chomsky put it, "tossing around the term conspiracy theory is a way to pooh-pooh institutional analysis." The fact is our economic institutions, political democratic institutions, and also many of our cultural institutions, including, glaringly, the mass media, have been taken over by a silent, creeping corporate coup.

What is shocking is that more people don't discuss it, although many do. Everybody knows it. But few dare to speak it. Many people, I believe, are simply shell-shocked, and behave like deer in the headlights, or rabbits, frozen stiff with a paralysis of fear, choosing the self-numbing option of denial and avoidance of the obvious and unsettling facts; and often engaging in magical thinking, telling themselves that the politicians and business elites, in whom they have lost all confidence, or someone else, will miraculously save us. This self-disempowering, self-deluding, quasi-messianic and regressive mode of thinking is extremely dangerous, as Erich Fromm and others have pointed out. Denial, and the disavowal of our power, our hearts and our common sense, is by now extremely perilous, and in fact deadly.

Not only have we been conditioned to be docile and deferential towards authority in our behaviour and our actions, but far worse, to defer to authority in our thinking, and to essentially mistrust our own judgement and common sense – even to the point of utter absurdity, of sheer insanity and self-delusion, denying what is right before our eyes. C. Wright Mills, Paulo Frère, Erich Fromm, Noam Chomsky and Henry David Thoreau, among others, have talked about this pattern and its great dangers. Such habitual and conditioned deference to authority leads naturally, furthermore, into a chronic state of denial of the obvious, to a denial of what is before our nose. *A chronic, conditioned attitude of self-disempowerment, leading to a docile acquiescence to power, and a denial of the very serious problems we all know to exist, is the single greatest problem we face, and the single greatest obstacle to creating a decent society, or any viable future for humanity. The sheep are in danger, and they are in danger precisely because they behave as sheep, and not as men and women.*

But this is changing, the denial is breaking, and the numbed state of paralysis is wearing off. Thankfully, the people are waking from what Eleanor Roosevelt called "a sleeping sickness of the soul." All around the world, the people are beginning to awaken, as even the intellectual in residence to the global elite, "Zbig" Brzezinski, lamentingly pointed out.

> *"Everybody knows that the ship is sinking.*
> *Everybody knows that the captain lied.*
> *Everybody's got that sinking feeling,*
> *like their brother or their dog just died....*
> *Everybody knows the deal is rotten;*
> *old black Joe's still pickin' cotton,*
> *for your ribbons and bows,*

and everybody knows...
Everybody knows that the dice are loaded... Everybody knows."

– Leonard Cohen

The emperor has no clothes. Democracy has been gutted by a pack of greed-driven corporate cannibals, who hide inside its rotting carcass, pulling sinews like strings on a puppet. No wonder the people tune out, and watch sitcoms or "reality TV" – reality is terrifying. Moreover, they are bored and disgusted by what they see in the arenas of power, and turn their faces away in revulsion at the banality of the evil they witness daily, in that box in the living room that connects them, however indirectly, and however much as mere passive spectators, as they are intended to be, to the fetid corridors of power, or at least their shadows and reflections.

The many turn their faces away, while the few rob and plunder the earth, and engage in an orgy of unrestrained greed, while destroying any future for humanity. But this is not the end of the story, much less the end of history. There is more day yet to dawn.

I've referenced and quoted Chomsky a number of times, not because I want to worship at his feet, not because he is infallible, which, by the way, emphatically, like everyone else, he is not, but simply because he has a lucidity and an understanding and a courageous honesty with regards to political-economy that is uncommon and unfortunately rare. He put it very plainly: *"If you want to understand a society, look at where power lies."* Pretty simple, straight-forward – should be obvious to everybody. And his answer, which any reasonably intelligent person should know by now: we live in a business-run society – the business elite own the country, and as George Carlin said, *"They own you."*

And the grand old dissident also quoted John Dewey, who said, *"Government is the shadow cast by business."* And he made the equally obvious remark, that *if you want to change the society, you don't focus all of your efforts on the shadow: you address the real powers, which are the economic structures and institutions, and the business elites who control them, and who own the country and most of the world.* (And you don't have to be a Marxist to realize this, or a leftist of any stripe – you just have to be reasonably sane, and not sleep-walking.)

To do otherwise is to engage in the kind of banal, although necessary, but almost idiotic rear-guard action that has come to pass for activism and progressive politics: a kind of battle-weary reformism that is constantly losing ground, and constantly yielding ground. That kind of "damage control" politics is vitally necessary, but we should recognize the facts and be honest with ourselves: the corporate rulers keep making gains, keep rolling back the gains won by people's movements over the past few hundred years, keep "leading" – or corralling – us into a dark, neo-Dickensian feudal era, keep hollowing out democracy and crushing human rights, civil liberties, freedom, and the power, solidarity, hope and voices of the people. *We are fighting an advancing forest fire with a garden sprinkler, and running backwards as fast as we can. A more serious set of strategies is undeniably and urgently needed.* Clearly what we are doing is not working. We need reform, we need damage control, and by now it should be plainly, even painfully obvious – we need a democratic revolution.

Chomsky was simply saying what is by now obvious to just about everyone, as the Occupy movement and the widespread, pervasive public indignation show: the business elite, the international corporate elite, have hijacked democracy and now effectively rule the world. Everybody knows this.

Look at the systems analysis that came out of Switzerland recently and was published in many places, including *Popular Science,* or *Popular Mechanics,* whichever it was, showing that a handful of about 40 corporations, mainly banks, control the world's economy – a case of science confirming the obvious.

Or look at the simple math, the simple figures: by 1994 the Fortune 500 biggest corporations controlled 60% of the U.S. economy – and concentration of wealth and real power has grown only staggeringly greater since then.

The IMF, World Bank, WEF and WTO, the CFR, Trilateral Commission and Bilderberg group, the Federal Reserve and the ECB are simply organizations that serve and are controlled by these same corporate elites, and these organizations are what the *Financial Times* called "the de facto world government." Everybody knows what's going on. It's a question of what we are going to do about it. If we decide not to decide, and simply drift with the tide, then we will end up with a very dark, neo-feudal era, in which all freedom and democracy have been destroyed, and the overwhelming majority of the people on earth are reduced to serfs, chattel, or slaves, while a tiny elite rules the world and devours both the planet and our future. If this sounds like an unpleasant future, and one we would wish to avoid, then we had better get very serious about looking at alternatives, and even more serious about taking action – and now.

Before discussing our options for a better world, or even a viable world, I'd like to make clear from the start as to what my views and values are, if that is not clear already. I believe in democracy. I believe that history has shown clearly and abundantly, that if you do not have democracy, you have tyranny of one kind or another. I believe in rule by the people, and in the people having the power to shape their own future – and not just in order to avoid tyranny, but also for the greatest happiness, creative self-empowerment and unfolding of the highest aspirations and potential of human beings.

It is not just a matter of material living conditions, of who gets what or how much: it is, even more importantly, a matter of freedom and empowerment, versus disempowerment, oppression and exploitation. The question of the distribution of power has always been more central, more pivotal, and more fundamental than the question of the distribution of wealth: while the latter is a critical matter of justice, the former is what decides the issue of the latter. We either have substantive, real democracy, or we have, not only tyranny and the absence of freedom, but also systemic injustice, and the oppression and exploitation of the many by the few. This, by now, is becoming very clear.

Unless freedom and democracy are real and present, human potential is thwarted and stifled, while tyranny grows, and crushes or suppresses the best in us all, and while the people and the earth are pillaged and robbed.

I believe in freedom, and in constitutionally protected rights and freedoms for all individuals. Tyranny of the majority, or by a ruling elite – either one – lead to the crushing of human rights and well-being for all: that is why constitutions and charters of rights and freedoms were created, and are vitally necessary to any just or decent society, now, or at any time.

I also believe that for democracy to be real, much less for justice and freedom to prevail, power must be held close to the people, and not in the hands of any kind of ruling elite – be it a banking elite, some other economic elite, a military elite, a religious elite or a political elite. *Over-concentration and over-centralization of power in society undermines authentic democracy, destroys all possibility of rule of the people, by the people, for the people, and opens the door to tyranny and oppression. If we wish for freedom, democracy or justice, then power must be kept close to the people.* (Thomas Jefferson was absolutely right on that point, while Thomas Hobbes was simply delusional, if not simply deceitful.)

In the mid- to long-term, personally I believe that some form of libertarian socialism is the best, freest and most just form for human society – where freedom, participatory grassroots democracy, voluntary mutual aid, sharing and cooperation are the foundations of our society. But we have time to debate that, so let no one get too agitated or flustered if they currently disagree.

In the short-term – *as in right now* – I would be happy with any government that seriously addresses the current hostile takeover by big business, that rejects that takeover, and that begins to restore power to the people; and to restore the rule of Constitutional rights and freedoms and of authentic democracy. If a Tory or Labour government, a Republican or Democratic government, a liberal, conservative, socialist or libertarian government, or any other truly democratic government (or coalition) were to advocate and take serious action to do just that, then I would support that government – and with great enthusiasm, despite other disagreements I may have with that government. *The central task of the moment is to restore democracy, and to re-take the power from the corporate elite who have usurped it, and to restore that power to its rightful place, which is in the hands of the people. All else is secondary to that most essential and imperative, most urgent task.*

In that spirit, for the purposes of restoring democracy and returning power to the people, I would be happy with a left-leaning social democracy, or a more centrist liberal democracy, or even a fiscally conservative libertarian Republican government – *so long as the new government is authentically and substantively committed to pushing back and rejecting the corporate takeover of democracy.*

This would mean that democratic government sets the limits on the banks and big corporations, controls the currency, and determines the policies of the government in order to serve all people, and not just the super-rich elite. It would mean the rejection and overturning of the current practice of allowing the banking elite and other corporations to determine government policy in their interests, and at the expense of both the people and the environment.

To start with, and as a minimum, we need democratic control over the currency, controls on capital flight, serious election financing legislation, and even more critically, serious anti-trust laws to prevent or break up excessive concentrations of monopolistic or cartel powers – *laws which are meaningful and substantive, and not hollow, and which are enforced;* the cancelling of NAFTA and other so-called "free-trade" agreements which in reality are corporate rights agreements, and strong regulations on the banking and financial industries in particular. Media reform, meaning, strong anti-trust legislation applied vigorously and unhesitatingly to break up the corporate media empires which now control virtually all the news, is also simply necessary and unavoidable, if democracy is to survive. Of course, any draconian, or in more honest terms, fascist legislation which has been passed – such as the Patriot Act and the Military Commissions Act – must be overturned and swept away, and rule by constitutional law and charters of rights and freedoms must be formally and authentically re-enshrined. Any democratic government that would support such minimum policies of a genuine populist constitutional democracy would have my support. You can call that government anything you like, but it would be a major step in returning real power to the people. It would be a step towards ensuring that democracy survives, and that democracy can thrive.

Whether a new and more genuinely democratic government is left-leaning or right leaning, liberal, conservative, democratic socialist or libertarian, so long as it is genuinely populist, democratic, dedicated to Constitutional rights and freedoms for all, and opposed in action and not just rhetoric to the current high-jacking of government and democracy by the transnational corporate elite, then I would happily support that government. It may be imperfect, but it would be a major step forward for the people, for it would be a step towards the safeguarding and renewal of democracy and the rightful power of the people.

Most essentially, what we must realize now is that in most countries, communities and regions, it will require a *coalition* of pro-democracy forces and movements coming from the grassroots populace, in order to defeat the ruling corporatist powers, and to restore and reclaim democracy, and make it real. *Sectarianism and partisan politics will guarantee the demise of democracy, the vanquishing of the people, and the consolidation of all power in the hands of the transnational corporate elite. The people must unite, or they will be devoured by a monstrous and insatiable, anti-democratic, anti-ecological and anti-human global regime. Make no mistake. It is unity, or it is defeat.*

In short, what I wish to see now is democratic revolution: a movement of the people to reclaim and restore their democracy, and to take the power back from the corporate and banking elite who have stolen it. Until this happens, nothing good can be accomplished on any significant scale, and the assault on freedom, democracy, civil liberties, the environment and the people, will continue, and will continue also to accelerate. This must be understood now, or we are lost.

The moment is near, if it is not here already: the people are fed up. Now is the time for *real change.* And to speak of real change, we must analyze the problems we face, and not take forever doing it, and also discuss visions for what kind of world, what kind of society, we would like to create to replace this teetering last empire of extreme corporate malfeasance and delirious, self-deluding overshoot. But in case there is any doubt as to the nature of the current global corporatist order, or any remaining hesitation with regards to vigorously and boldly addressing and *overturning* it in favour of a more real and genuine democracy, let us review a few key facts. Denial is sleeping gas; and sleeping gas is now a deadly poison to the people, and to all life on earth. Let us deal with reality, or reality will deal with us. Better we take the initiative – I guarantee you.

In a typical goldmine in Africa, 3% of the wealth produced stays in Africa, and 97% of the wealth is extracted from the country, and goes primarily to the already stratospherically rich Western and international business elite. I relate the example because it is an indicator of the "normal" pattern of the current state-capitalist, or global neo-feudal corporatist order. For every dollar of "aid" that flows into Africa, at least ten dollars of wealth flows out, and is extracted from the continent through capital flight and off-shoring of profits and earnings – or to put it in more starkly honest terms, Africa, like the rest of the world, is being systematically raped and pillaged by an insatiable, ravenous and indescribably gluttonous international business elite.

The tax haven island of Jersey alone hides $500 billion in extremely secretive private bank accounts and trusts, protecting the rich not only from paying taxes, but from investigation as to where the money came from and how it was gained: and Jersey is just one of a network of off-shore tax havens designed to hide money for the super-rich – money and capital which could be used to build schools, housing, health clinics and hospitals, green energy infrastructure, or other critically and urgently needed projects that would benefit human beings and the biosphere. Instead, it is used to fund extreme self-indulgence and excess for the few, while the majority of humanity is pushed further into poverty, and the biosphere is pushed further and further towards collapse.

The total amount of money and capital sitting in this global network of hidden accounts totals trillions of dollars. The current estimate is that $11.5 trillion in private accounts is hidden in these offshore banks and tax havens. A fraction of this amount would eliminate global poverty and build a green energy and transportation infrastructure for the world, thus solving the worst of our social problems while creating the basis for a sustainable society – a society that will not self-destruct, but which can survive beyond the next few decades, and even thrive.

Such figures are staggering, and very difficult to comprehend, as they are simply mind-bogglingly vast. To bring these numbers down into a context that we can readily understand, think about this. $1 trillion is 1,000 billion dollars. $1 billion is 1,000 million dollars. 1,000 x 1,000 is 1 million. So $1 trillion is equal to 1 million x $1 million dollars. $100 million is the cost to build a hydrogen highway for California. $100 million is the cost to build an advanced physics research centre in Waterloo, Canada. $50 million is a typical amount for a major, multi-decades, long-term infrastructure and development loan for an economically poor nation in the Global South. If we redistributed some of this wealth to give, not a $50 million loan, but a *$1 billion grant,* as a partial repayment for the decades and more of looting and pillage, to the poorest 200 nations on earth – which is more nations than there are existing, but just so we can use easily understood round numbers – for social and community needs and infrastructure, and not to line the pockets of the same transnational corporate elite, the cost would amount to 200,000 million dollars, which is $200 billion, which is one fifth of $1 trillion: which is 20% of one trillion, or just 2% of the total estimated holdings of the hidden accounts of the super-rich. We could give $10 billion to every country on earth for social and environmental needs, allocated on a community level so as to avoid corruption or misallocation, a total of $2 trillion devoted to the needs of the people and the environment, and still use only a fifth of this truly vast pool of wealth.

To further put this figure in context, consider that just $1 billion, out of this pool of $11.5 trillion, is enough to dig wells for a thousand villages and neighbourhoods, and provide water for everyone on earth who lacks it – roughly a billion people. That is just one ten thousandth of this ocean of wealth that is now being controlled by the 1% super-rich.

And we haven't even discussed the more than $24 trillion that was given to the banks in the form of bailouts – which, of course, the people should demand back, to be put to use for the benefit of the people and the earth, and not simply for the benefit of the banking elite and their cronies.

In total, if justice were done – *as it will be, and soon* – the people of the earth, just in these two networks of elite concentrations of wealth, would have access to more than thirty-five trillion dollars – far more than is needed to thoroughly transform this world, to eliminate all poverty, and to create the infrastructure for a green and truly sustainable society that can survive and thrive for generations to come.

Surely it is time for justice. This amassing of vast pools, oceans of wealth by a tiny elite, while the majority of humanity is pushed deeper into poverty, the environment is plundered and relatively little money is put into addressing it or resolving the crisis, and the middle class is disembowelled and decimated – this is beyond intolerable. There are no words for the atrocity of the situation or for the extreme avarice and brutality of this newest of empires under which we live, which is the global plutocracy of neo-feudal corporate rule.

The trillions of dollars recently given to the banks could have been vastly better spent paying off the mortgages of all Americans who are struggling financially, putting money into the hands of the middle class to truly and effectively stimulate the economy, *and* building affordable housing for those who lack it. Instead, Bush and Obama, along with other prostitutes to the banking elite, bowed to their masters on Wall Street, and handed them the remains of the Treasury – and the people allowed this to happen.

The problem is not a lack of resources, capital or money – the world is awash in capital, and the super-rich are swimming in money. The problem is the distribution of wealth, and the allocation and access to capital and resources, and even more critically, most critically of all, it is a problem of the distribution of *power* – the few rule the world while the people are systematically disempowered and democracy is gutted. We either restore democracy, or we forget about any hope for a better future, or any future at all. I don't know how much more clear this can be.

This is not a question of capitalism or socialism, by the way, and these terms are so pervasively misunderstood that it is probably best to avoid them for the moment. The central question is not left or right, but the *vertical* distribution of power. (See the Nolan Chart for a more intelligent picture of political dynamics and realities than the traditional, overly simplistic, one-dimensional left-right spectrum.) *The question is whether power is held either in a top-down, highly controlled pyramid structure, or whether power is held closer to the grassroots, in the hands of the people.*

Again, *the central question that we face as human beings today is not a question of left versus right: it is a question of democracy versus oligarchy, plutocracy, or rule by the super-rich.* (It is the vertical axis of the Nolan chart which is critical, the axis of power distribution, and not the horizontal axis which deals more with wealth distribution, which is important, but has always been derivative from the former, and in essence, is secondary to freedom and basic dignity.) *The rest can be debated later, once we have secured freedom, democracy and basic, fundamental human rights.*

We don't have capitalism in any case – we have *corporatism*, as defined, very accurately, by Mussolini. Remember what Nelson Rockefeller himself said: *"Competition is a sin."* The elites are first and foremost monopoly men – they want as much control and as little competition or hindrances to their power, their actions and their profits as possible. What they want is rule by cartel – which in political terms is called oligarchy or plutocracy, or corporatism, as defined by Mussolini, which he said is the proper name for *fascism*: and it is the antithesis of democracy or freedom.

The elite business class or oligarchs who rule the planet don't want free markets any more than they want democracy – they want control: they want an empire, a global empire, that is ruled by and for themselves. This must be clearly understood. This is not free market capitalism – as utterly dysfunctional, anti-democratic, anti-ecological, anti-human and even economically unstable and self-destructive as that has been proven to be, anywhere it has been attempted, as witnessed for example by the Chile experiment under Pinochet, which devastated both the economy and also the people; or in post-Soviet Russia, where free market capitalism was introduced, and the predictable result ensued, with a few individuals becoming billionaires, the emergence of gangster capitalism and pseudo-democracy, and the plummeting of living standards among the people by 40%, virtually overnight. The ruling corporate elite want massive government subsidies for themselves, which of course must come from taxing the people, so that the super-rich can effectively rob the people more systematically and more severely by the aid of the state. What they are far more concerned with, however, even above money and the continued hyper-accumulation and hyper-concentration of wealth in their hands, is power: they want to be all-powerful, so that they can do anything they want, and no one will be able to stop them, and even complaint will be silenced.

What we have now, and what the international ruling elite of bankers and other plutocrats want, is a highly controlled society in which they own and rule the world. *What we have, and what the corporate and financial elite want, and are actively, vigorously, daily pushing for further, is a kind of 21st century feudalism, with themselves as the new god-kings, and the rest of us reduced to peasants, or worse.* Such infantile dreams of grandiosity have always been smashed against the rocks of history, but that doesn't stop the ravenously greedy or megalomaniacal few from trying the same thing, generation after generation; and the harm that is done and the dangers created by these mad acts of imperial ambition, cannot be underestimated, nor left unchecked.

> *"Let's call it like it is – it's fascism."*
>
> *– Gerald Celente*

The few control the lion's share of the wealth of the earth, as well as the global economy, the farms, the factories, the media, the international economic and financial institutions, and also, generally speaking and with only a few exceptions, the politicians, the major political parties and the political process and governments of the world. The problem, as always, and increasingly so, is the extreme and rapidly growing disparity of wealth, and, more critically, of power, and the increasing hyper-concentration of wealth and *power* in the hands of a tiny and, by now, global elite. If this is not addressed, the future for humanity will most certainly be bleak.

There is no lack of wealth or money in the world. It is simply being hoarded, expropriated, siphoned off and gobbled up by the super-rich. The world order under which we live, this latest of empires, which is a transnational corporate empire run by and for the plutocracy of the world's billionaires, is nothing short of vampiric – as well as utterly self-destructive and completely unsustainable, economically as well as ecologically – and this is not the slightest exaggeration.

It is time for an end to the plunder, and for a radical redistribution of wealth as well as power. As Ghandi said, there is enough for everyone's need, but no one's greed. The US leads the world in the race to the bottom, in the race to see who can exploit the people the most, and create the most obscene and glaring disparity between the rich and the poor, and it seems that most of the world is intent on following the example. The richest 400 family dynasties now control more wealth than the poorest 100 nations and the majority of the world's people – while five billion people live in poverty and over 20,000 children die daily of hunger. This is beyond unjust.

There are no adequate words for such a state of affairs, other than *rape and pillage*. When 1% of the global populace is consuming or hoarding the majority of the wealth and resources, there will be great poverty, misery, conflict, war, crime, violence, ecological devastation and tremendous suffering for humanity. This is intolerable, radically unjust, and also completely unsustainable, and so, must end now.

Extraction and expropriation of wealth from every corner of the globe and all of humanity and the earth by the super-rich is the primary pattern of our current global social-economic order, and everything is geared to facilitate that global pillage – including the universally imposed neo-liberal political-economic structures, along with the general destruction of all barriers – *including democracy*, we should note – to a world-wide looting fest by the few who are already obscenely engorged.

The poor and middle class are taxed more and more, while the richest pay little or no tax, and are in fact massively subsidized by the state, which of course they control, through their bribery and manipulation of the politicians (which is euphemistically called campaign funding), and through the revolving door policy of corporate to government to corporate positions. Social and ecological programs can't be properly funded and are slashed further and further under "austerity measures" because the biggest corporations eat up the funds through massive state subsidies and tax breaks, and because the international banking elite siphon off extortionary levels of public funds to pay interest on debt that was incurred to "subsidize" the same corporate backers and masters of the politicians. *Whose* debt is it? It is the elites'. And I say, let them eat debt. It is theirs.

The "Washington consensus" of Chicago School, so-called "free market" or "free trade" neoliberal economics, also known as globalization, which is more accurately described as corporate feudalism, or simply, corporatism, has been, by all measures, a disaster for both humanity and the earth, with the corporate giants and the richest 1% benefiting enormously, while virtually everyone else loses. Even in terms of simple economic stability, it has been an undeniable disaster, with economic crises increasing in frequency and severity, and the entire global economic system at risk due to the unchecked greed of the few. Control over the economy, the productive capacities of nations and communities, and the wealth and resources of the earth have been further concentrated in the hands of the few. More than five billion people live in poverty, with poverty rising around the world. The poorest are cast to the streets, or to the garbage dumps in search of food, and when and if they do find work, they are ruthlessly exploited – and then they are typically blamed for all of the problems in society. The middle class is being devoured; the gap between the rich and poor is staggering, worse than at any other time in history, and is widening; and billions of people are struggling to survive, while the richest fraction of a percent of the world's population grows ever more astronomically wealthy, even while they already have more wealth than they could spend in lifetimes.

And all of this is in addition to the full frontal assault on democracy, human rights, civil liberties, freedom and the environment, which the ruling super-rich plutocrats are waging daily and relentlessly, in large part, in order to make sure that nothing and no one will stand in the way of their global feeding frenzy. Something clearly has to give. It is time for real change.

I think it is helpful to look at, not only what is wrong, what needs to be addressed, what problems we are facing – which is analysis – but also vision: what kind of society we would like to create, live in, work toward or see unfold. In that spirit, vision is very helpful. I would say essential.

We can be so engrossed in details that we can't see the forest for the trees; or we can lose sight of where we are going or what we are doing. Vision broadens and lengthens our view. Vision is contextualizing, and context brings clarity; and clarity brings increased power and effectiveness.

It is hard to inspire anyone, or even inspire ourselves, if we have no vision as to where we are going, or what we are trying to accomplish. Vision brings inspiration, and inspiration brings action, dedication, a rallying of support from the people, and a uniting of the people. Vision is therefore as essential as analysis – and probably even more so, for the people already have a sense of what is wrong: what is lacking is a vision of an alternative, a vision of a better way.

Vision rests upon and arises from our views and values. These we must clarify. Analysis clarifies where we stand now, as well as where we have been, and what we have experienced in the past. Both analysis and vision are essential to positive social change.

Saying that we will figure it out as we go is only a partial answer. Marx thought a better society would get worked out naturally as we went along, with no clear picture as to where we were going, and the Marxist experiment in Russia ended up as Bakunin predicted, with a worse form of tyranny than what it had opposed. Vision therefore cannot be ignored, brushed aside or by-passed. We must have a sense, a broad sense at least, not only of what we are against, but also what we are for. That means vision.

Connecting analysis and vision is strategy. Strategy is the art of getting from A to B. That may sound simple, but often it requires some considerable thought. Strategy is also essential, as are vision and analysis, but strategy will only be as strong and effective as our analysis and vision are clear.

Generally speaking, first come values, then analysis, then vision, then strategy: what do we value, where do we stand, where do we want to go, and how do we get there? These are the defining and highly important questions of values, analysis, vision and strategy, respectively.

Although we don't have to have everything perfectly worked out in our minds and perfectly clear in any of these aspects before we move on to the next, we do need them all, and they tend to rely upon one another in that same order of depth.

The foundation comes before the roof, when you are building a house; and the excavation comes before the foundation. Analysis first: dig. Digging means analysis. Then lay the foundation, which is vision. Strategy will follow from that. But this is only a general principle, and not a universal rule, of course. What we need above all is action.

There is no one single vision for humanity, if for no other reason than these simple facts:

1. Nobody has all the answers – no one is omniscient.

2. Human beings are diverse, in spite of our underlying unity and commonality.

3. Local and regional environmental and social conditions vary and are diverse.

4. Any monolithic or universalized vision turns into an oppressive tyranny of imposition, aggression, elitism, authoritarianism, colonialism, imperialism or simple arrogance and domination.

5. Life is change, and not everything can be planned in advance – we must learn and adapt as we go.

(The West, in its dire drive to excel and perfect and find something beyond what is, could learn profoundly important lessons from Taoism and Buddhism and the East generally, by the way, just as it could learn much from its own mystics, which are generally ignored. Hear Lao Tzu for a moment: *"Trust the people – leave them alone."* Or Chuang Tzu: *"A large nation should be governed as you cook a small fish."* (Gently.) Or Lao Tzu again: *"If you want to control the cattle, move back the fences."* And again, and most explicitly, *"The greatest danger is the excessive use of force."* For a Western correlation, see Thoreau, the natural Taoist of America.)

Having said that, and recognizing that there will be many visions for the future of humanity, it is worthwhile, I believe, to present our thoughts and ideas, to share them and to discuss them. Regionalism will also come into play. One group of people or one community, possibly one region or one nation, will opt for a certain vision or way forward; other groups, communities, regions or nations will adopt other visions or paths ahead. This diversity is a strength, for we can learn from one another as we experiment: this aspect worked well; this aspect worked not so well and needs to be modified; this other aspect was a disaster, and should be abandoned.

Regionalism is also more democratic than a homogenous one-size-fits-all, top-down approach: it is more aligned with the spirit of freedom and also creativity and innovation; and it gives humanity a greater resilience due to diversity, as well as a steeper learning curve, faster learning pace, since across the world, we are attempting various ways and means of doing things, simultaneously, and our understanding will be the richer for it.

Regionalism, plurality and diversity should therefore be core values we embrace while seeking ways to heal this world. Regionalism does not preclude *solidarity* or *mutual aid*: we can embrace both *unity* and *diversity* – the two are completely compatible, and also complimentary; just as freedom and compassion, or freedom and cooperation, are not at odds, but mutually reaffirming and mutually supportive.

Gradualism will also come into play. I know a lot of revolutionary-minded people don't like that word, which sounds like reform, or a general plodding slowness or timidity – and I never did either, until recently – but while I do believe we need a revolution, a non-violent democratic revolution, or a wave of them across the world, decentralized and locally or regionally-based, I think it is important for us to realize that we will not likely achieve the ideal civilization or form of human society in one fell swoop. Even with a revolution, it will be a work in progress. We may make certain bold and sweeping changes now, or at least very rapidly, and yet have many more steps or phases of transition ahead of us before we reach anything like the ideal state of society.

We are not so utopian that we think everything can be accomplished in a day. But we are bold enough and brave enough and imaginative enough to envision a better world. We can work towards a better world together, step by step. *Time is of the essence, and dragging our feet or resisting change is now very, very perilous, and therefore extremely unwise.* At the same time, pushing too aggressively, to the point of violence or rabid sectarian intolerance, ideological fixation or fetishizing, or being too perfectionistic, will only bog down the entire process of social change, and actually block our way, rather than advance our vision for a better world.

Rome wasn't demolished in a day, and this latest empire of global corporatism will not be overturned in a span of 24 hours, most likely. Even if it is, the process of building a better society will take time, and will not be finished overnight. Take a breath: we're in for the long haul, and a long-term vision is needed – almost as much as we need bold, immediate action.

As to a long term vision, for myself, I believe some form of libertarian communism is the ideal. This means, to my view, a community-based, participatory democracy, where sharing and cooperation are the basis of society. Cooperation is voluntary and not forced, and goods and services are shared freely – as adults would do, if we had any around: sharing and cooperation are things we were supposed to have learned in kindergarten. This should not be viewed, therefore, as an impossible goal.

To be fair, most people are more than decent, have basically good hearts, and are struggling simply to get by. The problem is not human nature: the problem is that in this corporate-dominated, corporate-run society, we are conditioned to behave like frightened, greedy little children, despite our natural basic goodness, and in spite of our common sense, both of which are systematically thwarted and suppressed. But we can rise above our conditioning and rediscover our truer nature. The best of us show the best in us, and not something foreign to our own nature. Moreover, we know this instinctively, at least on some level.

I agree completely with another statement by that typically lucid elder by the name of Chomsky: most people have basically decent impulses. There are, according to the studies, only about 1% of the population who are sociopaths, who have no real feelings of sympathy, empathy, compassion or caring for their fellow human beings. These people tend to gravitate to positions of economic, political or social power, so they can indulge their ruthless self-centredness, and the elite are composed of more sociopaths than simple inept morons and fools (intelligent non-sociopaths, people with good hearts and bright minds, tend to get weeded out naturally by a system of institutionalized greed, and the scum floats to the top). The rest of the population however, despite their faults, do have an instinct towards love, compassion, empathy, and helping one another.

Compassion, sympathy, empathy and cooperation are all natural, as the great Russian biologist, who is in truth the peer if not the superior to Darwin, Peter Kropotkin, also showed in his classic work, *Mutual Aid*; and which *Scientific American* also testified to in a recent article on natural reciprocity among primates; and which Jeremy Rifkin has written about, discussing the findings of science as to our natural empathy, in his book, *The Empathic Civilization.*

But while we are naturally, instinctively, warm of heart and inclined towards cooperation, reciprocity, peaceful coexistence, empathy, compassion and mutual aid, these natural human traits have been systematically suppressed and conditioned out of us by a society that is ruled by a system of institutionalized greed, and by overlords who want meek, alienated, atomized, unthinking and unfeeling consumers, cogs and mindless drones.

The ruling elite maintain their power by the primary method of divide and conquer, and bonds of love or human sympathy, empathy, compassion, caring, mutual aid or cooperation, threaten to unite the people, and a united people would quickly overturn and overthrow the power of these newest of emperors and tyrants. So they can't have that: they can't have people acting on their natural instincts of sympathy, solidarity, compassion or cooperation, and instead we are systematically conditioned, from birth and also daily, to be self-interested individualists, who pay lip service to our higher virtues while we vigorously pursue our narrow self-interests, shop till we drop, and bunker ourselves into an isolated cocoon lined with technological gadgets and simulated reality. *We live in a society that speaks of justice and compassion and love, and rewards callousness and greed. We are schizoid, and our deeper, better nature, is to some degree – fortunately not completely – covered over by layers of frankly harmful, self-deceiving and self-destructive social conditioning.* Our socially conditioned second nature is not in our best interests, nor the planet's, nor that of others. We must overcome it, and soon – and we can.

Greed and self-centredness, just like violence and hate, are childish, anti-social, and toxic to both ourselves and to one another – and we do have the capacity to rise above them. It is a matter of trusting ourselves and drawing out our natural instincts towards love, compassion, solidarity and mutual aid. It is not a matter of improving human nature: it is a matter of cutting through the social conditioning which has partially covered over our natural instincts towards compassion and cooperation, along with our basic intelligence. It is a matter, you could say, of liberating our natural basic goodness and innate common sense.

In a society characterized by libertarian communism, to return to the original discussion, power is held as close to the people as possible – not, of course, in some horrific totalitarian or even authoritarian or bureaucratic state, which was an utter failure as a human experiment, as Bakunin predicted. Power is held at the level of the community, so that no one person or group has power over others, and no one person, group or class can exploit or dominate another; and communities share information and goods freely among one another.

Most essentially, libertarian communism recognizes the dangers of excessive concentrations of *any* form of power in society, be it political, economic, military, religious or otherwise, and it values compassion and mutual aid as well as freedom, and aims to put these values into practice, and not just talk about them. Instead of having a class-based society where some are rich and many more are poor, wealth is shared. Instead of having wide disparities in the distribution of power, with some powerful and others dispossessed of their power, all are empowered, and domination is not permitted unless there is very good reason for it. For example, if your five-year-old daughter is running out into the street, you exercise a temporary domination or coercion to forcibly pull her by the arm back to safety – but generally, domination, like submission, is considered to be an anti-social, demeaning and degrading, dangerous tendency that must be guarded against, and rejected in favour of liberty, equality and solidarity – *the founding values of the Enlightenment*, which, I would suggest, we should reaffirm, *and live up to.*

Some will say this vision for society is naive, that we must have a powerful central government to protect people from harming one another – to protect the people from themselves. That was the argument of Thomas Hobbes, and modern society has been based ever since upon that fallacious and irrational argument, the product clearly of either sloppy thinking or self-serving deceit – an argument which Jefferson critiqued and laid to waste with a single sentence: "If you can't trust people to govern themselves, how can you trust them to govern others?"

Clearly, if you are sceptical and wary of human nature, you should avoid giving anyone, or any group, great power over others. Would this not be the most rational and sane, common-sense conclusion to draw? Of course it would – and our entire elitist, authoritarian, overly centralized, bureaucratic, technocratic, hierarchical social structure is built, therefore, upon a lie, and an illusion.

When we pierce the veil of that illusion, we will experience a freedom the likes of which we never thought possible, and justice will roll down like a mighty river. Until then, we are dwellers in a cave of shadows, more mice than grown men and women, and mild reforms are all we have the courage to imagine.

> *"None are more hopelessly enslaved than those who falsely believe they are free."*
>
> *– Goethe*

Some will say such a society, based upon freedom, sharing and cooperation, is unattainable, but as this is a long term vision, we probably have time to debate it, to mull it over, to give it some thought and some serious discussion – it's not likely to be the subject of a referendum next week. We have some time to think about it.

Those who say that a society based upon equality, freedom, solidarity, partnership, cooperation and mutual aid is impossible are, like Thomas Hobbes, utterly ignorant of anthropology, and of the longer sweep of our history. *The Ecology of Freedom* should be required reading for every high school student, along with *Mutual Aid* and *The Empathic Civilization*. If we do not know our history, we are doomed to repeat our worst mistakes, while remaining woefully unaware of our times of greatness, and our capacity for greatness.

I would say furthermore that it is not only naive but delusional to continue to believe that a society based upon unrestrained private greed, with a self-insulating, self-rationalizing, self-justifying plunder mentality among the ruling elite, is anything but radically self-destructive, as well as grotesquely unjust, tyrannical and anti-democratic, and at this stage of human history, simply terminal. The belief that this current world order not only should continue, but *can* continue, is beyond naive – it is wildly self-delusional. This order *will not* last – it will either be overturned by the people, in a global wave of democratic revolutions, or it will destroy itself, and most of life on the planet along with it.

But more importantly, it is not a matter so much for debate as for experimentation: why don't we see if such a social model as libertarian communism, or libertarian socialism works, by actually trying it, rather than presuming in advance that it is impossible. And it doesn't have to be all or nothing: we can test it out on small scale models before applying it across a nation or region, if we choose. Many such experiments have already been conducted, and are functioning now, and with considerable successes. The point is, however, that we need not confine ourselves to mere theory or speculation, which often rises no higher than presumption and very blinkered ideological dogmatism in any event. Experimentation is in alignment with the scientific method, with human creativity, and also with common sense. Closed-minded dogmatism is not.

There are religious fundamentalists, and there are secular fundamentalists. All ideologues are fundamentalists, and ideologues are blinkered fools, posing as sophisticated and intelligent human beings. They are neither of the latter – they are self-blinding, and make themselves, functionally, simple morons.

Clinging to assumptions is like clinging to rocks in a sack we drag behind us. Worse, it is clinging to mental walls that prevent us from seeing anything clearly, including what is before our nose.

Ideologues do not create positive change in human society – whether it be technological innovation, social innovation, new art or new ideas, nor any social improvements, such as the abolition of slavery, the universal right to vote, the recognition of the equality of men and women and all peoples, nor anything truly useful, generally speaking. Ideologues sit in the middle of the street and block the road, decrying any efforts to try something new or different.

"I don't know about that "wheel" thing you keep talking about – don't you think we do just fine, dragging things along the ground behind us? What are you, some kind of utopian dreamer? You're talking nonsense. It isn't possible. Your head's in the clouds. Next you're going to tell me we can fly, or go to the moon! No, wait, you're going to tell me that leeches and blood-letting are not effective medical treatment. What a lunatic! No, no, I know – you're going to tell me the earth *isn't* flat, and that it's *not* the centre of the universe! Kids these days!"

But we digress.

In the long term, we can discuss what kind of society we would like to see. We don't have to agree *right now, this instant.* Quick – give me an answer to all human social and ecological problems and dilemmas – you've got thirty seconds.....

Or maybe we can take a more sane approach, and realize that such questions require considerable thought, and not merely glib, flippant presumption.

Had human beings stuck with presumption, with the familiar and the "known," with what they assumed they already knew, and not used their imagination, we would literally still be living in caves, eating nuts and berries, and wiping our asses with fig leaves. Not that that would be so bad, but we have opened up the possibilities for human existence considerably since then, and I would argue that is a good thing.

Presumption is functional stupidity, and it is our greatest weakness and greatest folly, as well as our greatest peril. Imagination and reflection are what separate us from rocks and amoebas, and make life worth living.

I would say that the values of freedom and compassion are core to any decent society, and must be both balanced and integrated. Libertarian communism does that best, I believe, and libertarian socialism is the next closest ideal. Our present society espouses the values of freedom and compassion, along with community, democracy and other mom and apple pie values – but living up to them is an entirely different story, and we are a very long way from that.

As much faith as I have in the basic goodness and common sense of humanity, underlying all the illusions, the faults, and the social conditioning, which is not a faith but a knowing that is profound and unshakable, I doubt that people are ready for something like libertarian communism, which would require the actual practice of sharing and cooperation, and the embracing of our power in ways that are neither passive nor aggressive, and neither dominating nor submissive.

Small groups of people may be willing and able to practice and live by these values, if they are committed to bringing out the best in themselves and one another, with love, gentleness, patience, respect, and a non-aggressive, cooperative spirit of mutual dignity and mutual aid; and families and couples and close friends, right now, today, and not in some utopian or distant future, when they live together well, live by these values to quite a high degree: but society as a whole is probably not ready for such a mode of living, although, I would certainly love to be proven wrong.

We have been conditioned, socialized and trained in contemporary society, from the time we were born, to live as alienated and compliant economic individualists, to "look out for number one," and to live (sic) as compliant and deferential subjects of ruling powers, and as obedient worker cogs and consumer drones. Sharing and cooperation, therefore, although natural, run counter to our conditioning, and thus, as with the embracing of our power, are not always things that come easily.

We can work toward the unfolding of these natural virtues of our being, but the full flowering across humanity is likely some ways off. Sudden leaps of understanding and awareness, and sudden shifts of consciousness can and do happen, so you never know (see Prigogine, Kuhn, Lovelock, Gladwell and others); and there is a renaissance emerging now, across humanity;

but I still think the ideal society is yet somewhere in the future, and maybe not quite as near at hand as some may wish. In the meantime, we need to concern ourselves, not so much with the ideal, as with discovering simply a better way. It need not be perfect: it need only be an improvement.

Was the abolition of slavery the end of our cultural awakening? Or the end of racial segregation; or the universal right to vote? No, these were important and essential steps toward a more spiritually mature, aware and just society, but we still have much work yet to be done, clearly. Steps toward the ideals of freedom, compassion, justice, and the fuller flowering of democracy are necessary, and in all likelihood will come in steps and in stages. We are not at the end of history – Fukuyama et al are either mad or deceitful – and the present order of society is far from the ideal, or the best we can hope for. We should aim higher, and be bold. We are not aiming for perfection, but merely a greater embodiment of our better selves. Life is not about getting by. Life is about living.

As a mid-term goal, I would hope for, and do aim for, work to create and aspire towards a form of libertarian socialism. Not everything is shared, private property is still in existence, but the emphasis is on liberty, mutual empowerment and equality, and on giving what you can and receiving what you need, so that a certain fairly high degree of compassion and justice are the foundations of our society, along with the values of peace, ecological sustainability, non-violence and freedom. This is not as idealistic as libertarian communism, where everything is shared; and it is much less of a stretch in terms of changes from our existing mode of living. The benefits however, for each individual, family or community, and for all, would be – *will be* – enormous, in terms of material living conditions, and more importantly, in terms of quality of life. We would no longer live as alienated, isolated, worker bees and machines, narrowly pursuing our competitive self-interest at the expense of one another, but would experience work, community and life in richer, more fulfilling ways, and not just with more material security, justice and equality, which would also be attained.

The Spanish Revolution of '36 showed that such a decentralized social order, based in freedom, equality and solidarity – the founding values of the

Enlightenment – is completely viable, and also highly viable in advanced industrial, technological societies. This is not an anachronistic, agrarian pipe dream for a few people on an island, but a very present option for us today, right now, if we choose it.

Though some might not like the description, I would describe libertarian socialism, or one version of it, as a kind of Jeffersonian, grassroots, partici-patory democracy, where democracy is more vigorous than Jefferson had envisioned, and democracy is based at the level of the community, rather than the states, with federations of communities for their mutual protec-tion, peace and prosperity. Of course, added to this vision would have to be racial and gender equality, as well as environmental sustainability. What also must be added to call it libertarian socialism, or simply to make it just, is economic democracy. Hence, the people who work in a workplace, demo-cratically control that workplace. (Michael Albert and Noam Chomsky have excellent and lucid thoughts on this subject, but we are making only a brief introductory sketch here.)

So decision-making is based upon very localized, democratic, open, trans-parent and participatory community councils; alongside worker councils which are made up of representatives from each workplace, school or insti-tution. (Yes, that is a big change from the present, and that is the point – the present situation of society is far from ideal. And yes, big changes have occurred in the past – the emergence of even a rough and ready, gestational democracy in the 18th century, for example, was a big change, and a positive change, from the straight-forward feudalism which preceded it.)

In short, libertarian socialism is a vision of a further evolution of democracy: democracy becoming more rooted in the grassroots, so that power truly does reside with the people; and democracy being applied to the economy, so that the people are not dominated by economic powers that have not been adequately addressed and are therefore tyrannical, as is the case now. (Jefferson warned us of the dangers, and urged a bold response, 200 years ago, but we failed to listen.)

Communities then would form federations for mutual aid and security, but power would remain at the level of the community, and the community itself would value not only justice and compassion, ecological sustainability and peace, but also freedom.

But again, this is just one vision. Some regions or communities might embrace such a vision, or elements of it, while others will attempt something different. It is a big wide world, and there is room for many different ways of doing things, and many different experiments in what it means to be alive.

From my view, some form of libertarian socialism is the best near-term goal for humanity, while libertarian communism is the best long-term goal; but there are over two hundred nations on earth at present, thousands of states and provinces, many thousands of regions, and millions of communities. There is room for diversity, and diversity is an asset, and a strength, as well as a necessity and an inevitability of life.

What is needed, however, is a global commitment across humanity to the values of non-violence, freedom and democracy – otherwise, great powers and "great" empires will crush any attempts at diverging from their interests. We need a commitment to democracy or we will continue to live with empire, and all of the brutality, injustice, violence and domination that entails.

Whatever vision we may hold for the future of humanity, to quibble about what should replace the presently ruling global order – which is most undeniably corporate feudalism, corporatocracy, corporate oligarchy, plutocracy, or simply corporatism – is really to miss the point entirely. What matters is that we choose between, on the one hand, rule by the super-rich and a handful of their chosen lapdogs, which is the present social order for most countries in the world, or on the other hand, authentic democracy.

The path of continued obedience and passive, deferential compliance with a world order, an economy, a political system and a society dominated by a global cartel of the super-rich and their corporate and political tools, means two undeniable implications: it means the continued conscious and deliberate demolition and evisceration of democracy, and the civil liberties, human rights and freedom that go with it, along with the drowning of the interests and desires of the people under a sea of corporate spin and elite contempt for what the people actually want; and it means the continued suicidal race to maximize short-term profits at the expense of the earth's ecosystems and the future of humanity. If we are at all concerned with either, then we should oppose the current global corporatist order, and work towards the restoration or creation of genuine democracy, now, while we still can.

"I do not want to end without mentioning another externality that is dismissed in market systems: the fate of the species. Systemic risk in the financial system can be remedied by the taxpayer, but no one will come to the rescue if the environment is destroyed. That it must be destroyed is close to an institutional imperative. Business leaders who are conducting propaganda campaigns to convince the population that anthropogenic global warming is a liberal hoax understand full well how grave is the threat, but they must maximize short-term profit and market share. If they don't, someone else will."

"This vicious cycle could well turn out to be lethal. To see how grave the danger is, simply have a look at the new Congress in the U.S., propelled into power by business funding and propaganda. Almost all are climate deniers. They have already begun to cut funding for measures that might mitigate environmental catastrophe. Worse, some are true believers; for example, the new head of a subcommittee on the environment who explained that global warming cannot be a problem because God promised Noah that there will not be another flood."

"If such things were happening in some small and remote country, we might laugh. Not when they are happening in the richest and most powerful country in the world. And before we laugh, we might also bear in mind that the current economic crisis is traceable in no small measure to the fanatic faith in such dogmas as the efficient market hypothesis, and in general to what Nobel laureate Joseph Stiglitz, 15 years ago, called the "religion" that markets know best -- which prevented the central bank and the economics profession from taking notice of an $8 trillion housing bubble that had no basis at all in economic fundamentals, and that devastated the economy when it burst."

*"All of this, and much more, can proceed as long as the Muashar doctrine prevails. **As long as the general population is passive, apathetic, diverted to consumerism or hatred of the vulnerable, then the powerful can do as they please, and those who survive will be left to contemplate the outcome."** [Emphasis added]*

– Noam Chomsky, Who Owns the World?

"Most of the media pays remarkably little attention to what's happening. Coverage of global warming has dipped 40% over the last two years. When, say, there's a rare outbreak of January tornadoes, TV anchors politely discuss "extreme weather," but climate change is the disaster that dare not speak its name."

"And when they do break their silence, some of our elite organs are happy to indulge in outright denial. Last month, for instance, the Wall Street Journal *published an op-ed by "16 scientists and engineers" headlined "No Need to Panic About Global Warming." The article was easily debunked. It was nothing but a mash-up of long-since-disproved arguments by people who turned out mostly not to be climate scientists at all, quoting other scientists who immediately said their actual work showed just the opposite."*

"It's no secret where this denialism comes from: the fossil fuel industry pays for it. (Of the 16 authors of the Journal *article, for instance, five had had ties to Exxon.) Writers from Ross Gelbspan to Naomi Oreskes have made this case with such overwhelming power that no one even really tries denying it any more. The open question is why the industry persists in denial in the face of an endless body of fact showing climate change is the greatest danger we've ever faced."*

"Why doesn't it fold the way the tobacco industry eventually did? Why doesn't it invest its riches in things like solar panels and so profit handsomely from the next generation of energy?"

"Part of it's simple enough: the giant energy companies are making so much money right now that they can't stop gorging themselves. ExxonMobil, year after year, pulls in more money than any company in history. Chevron's not far behind. Everyone in the business is swimming in money."

*– Bill McKibben, "Why the Energy-Industrial Elite Has
It In for the Planet"*

Humanity is now in danger of crossing a threshold of no return. We have set into motion, and continue stubbornly to set in motion, causes and conditions which are destroying the basis of life on this planet. If we do not make major changes very soon, we will cross a threshold at a certain point in the not too distant future where the causes we have set in motion will become irreversible, to the effect that we will have guaranteed our own extinction. We are not there yet, but we are rapidly approaching such a line in the sand, a line of extinction that we will have drawn for ourselves.

In short, we must make major changes in our society now, or we will cross that threshold of no return, and humanity will go extinct, and there will be no future of any kind for the children of humanity. If this does not motivate the most callous or reality-avoidant of hearts, I sincerely do not know what will.

And all the evidence makes it abundantly clear, that the changes which are urgently needed in the world today are not going to come about so long as a handful of corporate giants and business elites dominate the economy, the financial system and the political process, and effectively rule the world. *Simply put, democratic revolution is now a matter of survival. And time is running out.*

We can debate until we are blue in the face what kind of democracy we should have – liberal, conservative, democratic socialist, libertarian socialist, etc. – but for both social and ecological reasons, *any* form of authentic democracy is vastly preferable to rule by a self-serving, rape and pillage corporate oligarchy of billionaires, intent on devouring the planet. *If we cannot get clear on this point, then we are lost, and our sentence to slow death is written by our own hand.* We had better get clear on this most crucial point, and right now. The clock is ticking, and reality is about to bite us in the face.

I would strongly assert, however, that while *a renewal of democracy is the one pivotal task of this century if humanity is to survive,* that in addition to democratic state power being captured (either through election or through revolution) by a truly democratic popular coalition, as opposed to the current norm of rule by a coalition or party of loyal servants to the plutocrats and corporate elite, *we need to look to practical ways of shifting real power back from the corporate and business elite, to the hands of the people.*

There has been much hew and cry and dismissive, scornful pooh-poohing over the Occupy movement not expressing a sufficiently detailed platform, proposal, agenda or vision. While such criticisms really miss the point – that the people know very well what is going on, and know that they are demanding a return of democratic power to the people from the corporate elite who have stolen it from them, who have usurped far too much power and greatly overstepped their proper bounds – we can say that a more crystallized vision is both helpful and indeed needed.

Well, if you want a vision, a platform, a concrete proposal for a better alternative, and a better world, here is one. And note that we are talking about the very near term – *as in, now.*

For any movement or effort which aims at restoring power to the people and renewing democracy to be truly meaningful and effective, and not just a hollow gesture, it needs to include the following, I would strongly advise. Among the necessary steps that must be taken if power is truly to be returned to the people – that is, if the corporate and financial elite are to be effectively dethroned and democracy reclaimed and renewed – are these: reigning in the banks, financial institutions and big corporations; making firm rules that they must abide by; forcefully removing the heads of the financial and corporate elite from the public trough; and eliminating the massive subsidies and bailouts which total hundreds of billions of dollars, and often trillions of dollars, which they now continue to receive, at the expense of the public purse, and at the expense of social and environmental programs and the people themselves – instead of giving $100 billion a year in tax breaks to large, profitable corporations, *not counting hundreds of billions and trillions in subsidies,* put $100 billion a year into small business and community economic development, and watch employment soar and the economy boom, and be transformed, in eighteen months or less; halting imperial warfare and ending the war economy, and shifting the massive savings – hundreds of billions of dollars a year in the case of the U.S. – to human needs; re-assigning much of the present military and "security" personnel to disaster relief, infrastructure development and restoration, building homes, schools and clinics, and other social and ecological needs; shifting public money away from serving the ultra-rich and the corporate giants and toward the needs and interests of the people – small business, community economic development, real jobs programs, housing, education, health care, infrastructure, green energy and the environment; shifting the tax burden off the poor and middle class, small farmers and small business, and making the billionaires and large corporations pay a fair share – 40% would be a reasonable minimum figure, considering the billions of dollars they are awash in; instituting a Robin Hood tax or Tobin tax on all financial transactions in order to reign in currency speculation and stabilize currencies and economies; instituting capital controls, particularly controls on capital flight and off-shoring of profits and earnings. Far more critically, control over the currency and the production of money must be held by democratic nation states, otherwise, there will be no possibility for either sovereignty or democracy whatsoever. As has been said before, if a nation does not control its own currency, through the power of democratically elected parliaments, then all talk of sovereignty or democracy is idle and futile. The banking elite certainly know this, as did U.S. presidents Jefferson, Lincoln and Jackson: it is high time for the people to realize it as well.

Other essential and urgently needed measures to renew and restore real democracy include instituting *real anti-trust legislation with real teeth*, to prevent or to break up cartels and excessive monopolistic or oligarchic concentrations of economic power, which always undermine democratic power as well as harming the people in more direct ways.

Parcel off 60 to 80% from the giants into worker-owned or community-owned co-ops, increasing economic diversity and competition and strengthening the economy as well as aiding the people – start with the banking, media, insurance, utility, transportation, resource and energy industries, for example.

Instituting anti-trust legislation in particular with regards to the financial industry and banks is becoming undeniably necessary and vitally urgent – too big to fail is nonsense and insanity, and means too big to exist: break them up now.

Anti-trust legislation is even more urgently needed with regards to the giant media empires than the banks: *a diverse and democratic media is essential to democracy, and must be forcibly created, if need be, by dismantling and breaking up the existing media empires* and parcelling out some of their giant and excessive holdings to locally owned and democratically controlled community media co-ops. The media workers know how to run the presses. The media empires need to be broken up, for the common good, and for the survival of democracy.

Six corporations control over 90% of broadcasting and print media in the U.S. In Canada, the situation is even worse. Break up the media empires and create networks of diverse, democratic, community-owned media co-ops. Now. This is democracy's oxygen. Democracy is not possible unless there is both media diversity, and also, broad-based citizens' access to the production and distribution of media, and not only to its consumption.

We also need the formal restoration of constitutional rule and charters of rights and freedoms, unfortunately, and the overturning and abolition of all anti-democratic, draconian or literally fascist "anti-terrorist" or "security" legislation, and a renewed dedication to constitutional rule, civil liberties, human rights and freedom.

We need election finance reform with serious teeth. We also must institute proportional representation in the electoral systems of the U.S., Canada and Britain, and everywhere it does not yet exist, as most European countries have done, so that elections can have at least some resemblance to actual democracy, and not simply endorse elite rule by dominant, corporate controlled parties, such as the Democratic and Republican, Liberal, Conservative and Labour Parties.

And the IMF and WTO need a slap on the nose with a rolled up newspaper, and to be told in a firm and uncompromising voice, backed by clear and unequivocal policy resolutions, effectively to back off. Democratic governments must control financial institutions, and *not* the other way around – *this is crucial for us to understand, and to demand.*

So-called "free trade" agreements must be assessed individually to see if they actually benefit the people, or, as with NAFTA and most other such agreements, they are in truth corporate rights agreements, which benefit transnational business elites and the biggest corporations, while severely harming everyone else, not to mention democracy and the environment: when they are the latter, as they usually are, they need to be cancelled and annulled, and immediately so.

Currencies, to be stable, need to be backed by something real (gold and silver seem most practical); and certainly *not* by the current global currency reserve, which is the U.S. dollar, which itself is backed only by a charade, by a shell game, by the printing of money out of thin air, and by the crumbling house of cards which is the U.S. Treasury, and which is a currency that is guaranteed to implode, and sooner rather than later.

What you certainly don't want to do is to put a cabal of bankers in charge of the printing and creation of the nation's money – that would be complete madness, and would of course sooner or later bankrupt the country, as well as undermining and ultimately destroying the sovereign democratic power of the people's government, *as Jefferson, Jackson and Lincoln knew very well, and fought with all their might to prevent - two of them being shot for it.* But of course, that is exactly what the U.S. did in 1913 with the creation of the privately owned central bank that became named the Federal Reserve, and other countries have followed the same insane policy. Clearly, this must be reversed.

Patent laws must serve the public good, and not merely narrow private interests – for example, the pharmaceutical companies, with their killer profits; and patents must cease to allow the expropriation of what are legitimately public domains of the commons, including especially, seeds, which are the basis of 80% of world food production. (Allowing control over seeds – and hence over agriculture and world food production – to be gathered in the hands of half a dozen transnational corporations, is a recipe for unprecedented disaster, as well as tyranny, since these companies will hold the power of feast or famine. Look up the Rockefeller/ Monsanto "doomsday vault" in Norway for a chilling forewarning of the dangers.) In most places, the minimum wage needs to be raised, and raised significantly; not lowered. Labour organizing rights must be re-enshrined and vigorously protected. Supply lines and economic dependencies must be shortened and diminished, and local economic development made a priority. Dependency on big oil, gas, coal and nukes must be drastically reduced, and control over energy supplies must be shifted to democratically controlled, community-based and community-owned green energy. Finally, and perhaps most essentially, the granting of the legal status of personhood to corporations, which was a disastrous error and an insane, thoroughly irrational and profoundly dangerous idea, must be immediately overturned.

These, I would say, are the minimum steps which need to be taken to restore power to the people, renew democracy, and protect it from further evisceration and destruction at the hands of the now reigning anti-democratic, anti-ecological, reckless and suicidal, global corporate and financial elite. If we care to deal with reality, then these steps are, by now, unavoidable.

The rightful power of the people to govern themselves through genuine citizens' democracy, has been usurped and stolen by a handful of robber barons and corporate elites. *Two hundred years ago Thomas Jefferson saw this, and warned us of this danger. But we refused to listen, and instead, gave in to the awful power of denial.* The corporate high-jacking of our democracy and our world has now become so blatant, so obvious, so undeniable, so brazen and extreme, that by now, virtually everyone can see it. The question of course, is what we are going to do about it?

What is needed is for a popular coalition – a genuinely grassroots coalition of the people, or a populist democratic movement – to reclaim power from the ruling corporate elite and their political cronies. The implementation of the necessary changes could then be made swiftly, in as little as a year, and our society would be transformed. Full employment, economic prosperity, a shift towards true ecological sustainability, justice, equality and peace, and a renewal of human rights, civil liberties, freedom and democracy, are just some of the benefits to such a bold and necessary course of action by the people.

And we don't *request* that the power be returned to the people by the ruling oligarchs and plutocrats – we take it. We take the power back. It is time for the people to reclaim their rightful democratic power. Dark age ahead, or renaissance? The power is in our hands to decide. And delay or indecision now, would likely be nothing short of disastrous.

Are we serious about democracy, freedom, justice, prosperity, ecological sanity or a future for humanity, or are we willing to allow a further slide into a dark age of neo-feudal, plutocratic rule by a rabidly anti-democratic, self-serving and ecologically suicidal global corporate elite? These are our present alternatives. Only fantasy presents a third option.

The moment of decision is now. There is no further time for vacillation, pro-crastination, hesitation, obfuscation, denial, or waiting to see what happens next. We know what direction we are being "led" in. The writing is on the wall. It is time for decisive action. The 1% must be dethroned, for either justice or democracy to prevail, or for there to be a future for humanity. (In actuality, it is a fraction of 1% who rule, but we understand the meaning.)

I realize, with some sadness, that I am speaking here to only a portion of humanity, to that portion which is not so terrified or numbed by our present realities that they cannot seriously contemplate in earnest the situation we are now facing. What I do trust, and know, is that the boldest, most imagina-tive and bravest of hearts, can and will lead this society, as they have always done. It is a delicate balance: lead without imposition, and not by aggres-sion or domination, but by inspiration, by showing what is possible. The timid will follow. That is the sad fact. They should lead too, but they refuse. They will find their time. In the meantime, this world needs healing, and the overly passive will not do it, so those who are willing, must.

If we are serious about restoring and renewing, or even safeguarding democracy, freedom or justice, then these steps will be taken, and swiftly, without delay, in order to return the power to the people. The majority of the people in North America, Europe and many parts of the world now support such a democratic shift in power and priorities, and such a renewal of democracy. What is needed is the boldness to create the grass-roots citizens' movements and broad-based popular coalitions that will seize democratic power and throw the plutocrats, the corporate oligarchs and their political lapdogs to the side – by any *non-violent* means necessary. There are many ways this can be done. Movement building and coalition building are the starting points, and fortunately, this is already well under way.

As for short-term goals, to make it as clear as possible what I believe we now need, I would like to see a wave of democratic revolutions arise around the globe, and restore power to the people, removing the corporatocracy (the plutocracy really) from power. This is not only possible – it is, in fact, emerging now.

After successfully accomplishing a democratic revolution in at least a number of countries – eventually all countries, but at least a few to begin with – we can look toward what we will institute in place of the neo-feudal corporatism that has been dethroned and rejected. Hopefully we will have a fairly clear vision, at least of basic principles, before this moment arises. A fully articulated plan is not necessary, although it may be helpful, as long as we are not rigid about it, and turn it into a cause for division, and hence failure to accomplish anything. We do need at least a rough outline or vision of what kind of society we would like to create, what values we want to be the guiding principles of a better society, and what we would like to replace the extremely unjust, anti-democratic, and suicidally anti-ecological present order of trans-national corporate rule. We need not wait until we have every detail worked out before we act, however. We need to act now, in fact, or there will be no future for humanity of any kind. *Knowing our values and our power, and the urgency of the time, is more than enough to make a bold start to an unfolding process of democratic revolution and renewal.* If Thomas Jefferson or Thomas Paine were alive today, they'd be commending the 99% movement, and asking those of us who are still sitting on the sidelines what we are waiting for.

Whether democratic revolution happens at the level of the nation-state, or whether in some cases nation-states break up into regional units, where some regions go independent under democratic revolution, and some remain with the old order in a shrunken scale, in whatever fashion it arises, we need democratic revolution now. It must be global, and it must also be local: that is, it must be decentralized, multi-faceted, pluralistic and diverse, as well as globally networked. There will be no single democratic revolution that arises and succeeds – and if there is one single monolithic revolution, you can be assured it won't be democratic. Diversity, again, is a strength, not a weakness. Where there is no single head, the head cannot be cut off, bribed or co-opted.

For democracy to be restored or attained, the power must be returned to the people. This cannot happen if power is far removed from the people. Bringing power close and into the hands of the people, means, therefore, a federated and decentralized approach, based in diversity and solidarity.

Different nations and different regions will have different approaches, styles, strategies and visions. The common theme will be, and must be democracy: restoring power to the people, or bringing real power to the people for the first time. The variations on this theme will be many, and the control of the movements for democracy must come from the bottom up.

The Occupy movement, the World Social Forum, the popular movements in Greece, Burma, Iceland, Argentina, Egypt and Tunisia, along with many other efforts, offer working examples to draw upon, however gestational these may be. Life itself is a work in progress. We can and must be bold. Our future depends upon it.

If we want philosophers, thinkers, writers or activists to call upon for inspiration or ideas, which I would say is very helpful, I would list these as a few sources among many for useful ideas: Chomsky, Bookchin, Rocker, Bakunin, Kropotkin, Bertrand Russell, Aldous Huxley, George Orwell, Emma Goldman, Helena Norberg-Hodge, Rianne Eisler, Joanna Macy, Joseph Campbell, David C. Korten, Étienne de La Boétie, Paulo Frière, Erich Fromm, Thomas Jefferson, Proudhon, Thomas Paine, Ghandi, Martin Luther King Jr., Emerson and Thoreau. None of them have all the answers, of course, but all have very good ideas and inspiring words for helping us to build a better world.

Most importantly, there will be no democratic revolution, *and therefore no future for humanity,* if we do not unite the people. If we want to work side by side only with people who agree with us, then we're doomed.

The corporate elite will continue to eat us alive, and to destroy every last remaining shred of both democracy and freedom, while continuing to destroy the planet and any future for human kind, unless we, the people, unite now.

What we have to agree upon most essentially, is that constitutional democracy is preferable to fascism, or to corporate rule. If we can get together on that, then we can restore and renew democracy, and make it real. Then, afterward, we can debate the myriad other issues we face.

First, we must reclaim our power, and take the power back. First, we need to unite the people, and to reclaim democracy. That is our only hope. We had better get started, or redouble our efforts.

In particular, we need to build a broad-based, grassroots popular movement to restore democracy. Everything hinges upon that.

Put your differences aside for the moment. We need to reclaim democracy, and only the unity of the people will make it happen.

Hold your nose if you have to, learn to relate with tolerance when we don't agree on everything, but get together, and unite the people now! This is our only hope.

The immediate goals, I would say, are to *inform, inspire, empower and unite the people* – beginning with ourselves. All that we wish to achieve will arise on that basis, and no other.

JTR
February 15, 2012

MARX, HEGEL, INDEPENDENCE AND REVOLUTION:
THOUGHTS ON ECONOMIC CRISIS, GLOBAL CORPORATE RULE, AND THE COMING RENAISSANCE

ELECTORAL POLITICS IN MOST countries today are largely a distraction from the real power struggles that are going on, both in the streets and behind closed doors. But grassroots politics, by contrast, have the potential to burst into revolution, and bring about much-needed, urgently needed social change – even while elections drone on, largely meaninglessly, rubber-stamping one or another of the candidates of the super-rich. This was the beginning thought for a conversation that made the hamster on the wheel get his little feet moving briskly in my head this evening.

A friend was mentioning the Scottish independence movement, along with a series of other, typically lucid thoughts that she is known to humbly share, and the conversation sparked these reflections, which, if I may, I will now share with you. Hopefully they are of some interest, and maybe even some help in this dangerous, troubled, yet exciting and hopeful time.

I don't know anything about the Scottish independence movement, other than that it is alive and strong, and has more hope now than in the time of Robert the Bruce and William Wallace. It sounds very interesting, and maybe also very promising.

The media pundits and talking heads all line up to sing the same chorus of course, decrying independence movements generally, and anything that might save national democracies from their present trajectory of further and ultimate evisceration at the hands of transnational global corporate interests; and virtually all of them sound like parrots of Thomas Hobbes – who Thomas Jefferson critiqued in a single sentence with all the lucidity needed to dispel the entire nonsensical line of thought: "How can you trust people to govern others if you can't trust them to govern themselves?" Hobbes was a self-deceiving lunatic, or else a professional liar, justifying excessive powers for the ruling elite by irrational if not disingenuous arguments and rationalizations: and the pundits, like the politicians, follow him still. Better they blindly follow Jefferson if they are to blindly to follow anyone at all – but that is impossible, for their habit is to defend and succour favour from power, not to critique and challenge it. Eliminate the unconscious Hobbesians from the media, and the air waves would be virtually silent.

Greece and Italy showed what happens with staying in the EU: bend over and let the bankers sodomize you, while picking your pocket and sucking the lint from your navel – all the while telling you it's for your own good.

As Gerald Celente said, "The money-changers have taken over. That's all this is about."

> *"Recent events in Greece and Italy have created more skepticism of the West's claim to be democratic. Two elected European prime ministers, George Papandreou of Greece and Silvio Berlusconi of Italy, were forced to resign over the sovereign debt issue. Not even Berlusconi, a billionaire who continues to lead the largest Italian political party, could stand up to the pressure brought by private bankers and unelected European Union officials.*

Greece's appointed – not elected – prime minister is Lucas Papademos, He is a former governor of the Bank of Greece, a member of Rockefeller's Trilateral Commission, and former vice president of the European Central Bank. In other words, he is a banker appointed to represent the banks.

Italy has formed a second democratic government devoid of democracy. The appointed prime minister, Mario Monti, doesn't have to face an election until April 2013. Moreover, according to news reports, his "technocratic cabinet" does not include a single elected politician. The banks are taking no chances: Monti is both prime minister and minister of economics and finance.

Monti's background indicates that he represents both the EU and the banks. He is former European advisor to Goldman Sachs, European chairman of the Trilateral Commission, a member of the Bilderberg Group, a former EU Commissioner, and a founding member of the Spinelli Group, an organization launched in September 2010 to facilitate integration within the EU, that is, to advance central power over the member states.

One interpretation is that the banks, which were careless in their loans to governments, are forcing the people to save the banks from the consequences of their bad decisions.

Another interpretation is that the European Union is using the sovereign debt crisis to extend its power and control over the individual member states of the EU.

Some say that the EU is using the banks for the EU's agenda, and others say the banks are using the EU for the banks' agenda.

Indeed, they may be using each other. Regardless, democracy is not part of the process.

There is little doubt that European governments, like Washington, have been financially improvident, living beyond their means and building up debt burdens on citizens. Something needed to be done. However, what is being done is extra-democratic. This is an indication that Western elites–the Trilateral Commission, the Council on Foreign

Relations, Bilderberg Group, the EU, transnational corporations,
oversized banks, and the mega-rich–no longer believe in democracy.

(In fact, the majority of the elite never did.)

Perhaps future historians will conclude that democracy once served
the interests of money in order to break free of the power of kings,
aristocracy, and government predations, but as money established
control over governments, democracy became a liability. Historians will
speak of the transition from the divine right of kings to the divine right
of money."

– Former associate editor of The Wall Street Journal,
Paul Craig Roberts

Canadian poet Bruce Cockburn said it best in his song, "Call It Democracy" – a must-listen for all who want to understand the global economy and the current corporatist world order. The IMF, the International Mafia Federation, as leading trend analyst Gerald Celente calls it, is *not* a friend of the people – nor are the international banking elite that control it. This is a frankly criminal network of thieves in high places, using financial hegemony and other methods to extract pound after pound of flesh from the people, until they are completely bled dry, and the bankers rule the world. Oh wait – that's what we have now.

Most of the politicians are Quislings, eager collaborators with the corporate overlords and the banking elite, and have no more scruples than sewer rats. Those with heart, intelligence and courage are generally shut out by a system that is ruled by and for the super-rich. If you're not a billionaire, you don't matter – more importantly, if you're not a loyal servant to the richest and most powerful of the multi-billionaires, you are silenced. These are the simple rules of our current global order of world-wide plutocracy: the history and nature of empire is not very imaginative, nor are the present hegemons and would-be Tzars. Their lack of imagination is their blind-side, and will be their downfall, but for the moment, we still have global corporate rule, rule by the super-rich plutocrats, and an all-out war on democracy, the people and the earth. Action must be taken.

If a popular movement has succeeded in creating a movement anywhere in the world that can potentially lead the people out of this morass that is rapidly descending into a neo-Dickensian, technocratic, neo-feudal dark age run by the banking elite and their cronies, and into some form of genuine democratic independence, then that is the only light at the end of the tunnel, and the only hope. We should be supporting such movements, wherever they arise, not dismissing them as throw-backs to a now irrelevant past. Democracy is not a fashion to be dispensed with, but an essential necessity for a decent, just and sane society – now or at any time. You either have democracy, or you have tyranny of one kind or another. Take your pick.

"Disobedience, in the eyes of anyone who has read history, is man's original virtue."

– Oscar Wilde

Of course, not everything is as it seems on the surface, or as it is presented to the public through that spin-box in the living room we call the TV. We should be careful not to assume that just because some political phenomenon in some country or countries is branded by the media as a people's movement, a popular movement, an independence movement, a popular rebellion, or as the heroic efforts of "freedom fighters," doesn't mean that it is so. The mass media is controlled by the corporate giants, of course, and the other major part of the mass media is owned or controlled by governments, which are in turn controlled by the same corporate empire. When the media therefore portrays Nicaraguan Contras as freedom fighters, and Al Qaeda fanatics in Libya as glorious rebels against tyranny, we should be sceptical. There are genuine popular movements, and there are fringe groups that are branded as popular movements, but which are front groups for the CIA, U.S. State Department or some other tool of imperial aggression. The Libyan rebels and the Contras are just two examples of puppet groups that were or are armed and funded by the CIA and its imperial allies. The Taliban during the Afghanistan-Soviet Union war were another example of rabid, militant, thoroughly anti-democratic CIA puppets that were painted as freedom fighters by a compliant corporate-controlled media – until the game changed, the needs of empire shifted, and they had to be painted as the next thing to Hitler. The "peaceful protestors" in Syria that are hailed by the same corporate media are in fact armed and funded by Washington, for reasons of empire, and certainly not for the goals of freedom or democracy. The examples go on and on: puppets to empire are presented as great heroes; opponents of empire are vilified, bought off, killed off, or bombed into oblivion – either physically or financially. But there are genuine pro-democracy people's movements out there of course, and they are all around the world, and growing, and deserve our support. The alternative is grotesque, and also bleak; and the current trend, if not stopped, will mean the end of both freedom and democracy, and with them, all human rights and all hopes for a decent future for humanity.

The current movement towards further and further hyper-concentration and centralization of power in the hands of fewer and fewer people, is the road to fascism and tyranny. If that is not yet clear, please take another look. It will be clear soon enough, I warn you, if it is not clear yet.

Democracy and freedom require that power be kept close to the people, as Jefferson well understood, and not overly centralized or removed from them by any kind of elite. The current thrust in Europe and North America, as with many parts of the world, is toward further concentration and centralization of power in the hands of an elite (the financial elite and their cronies), and that spells the end of democracy and of freedom – as well as justice and well-being for the many – if we do not halt the trend.

Independence for Scotland would be very rough, at least initially, but staying in the UK would most likely mean a continued slide from desolate corporate rule into outright corporate fascism. The moves the EU took to put the bankers in overt government in Italy, show that staying in the EU means the same. The EU has now proven its fierce allegiance to the banking elite, at the expense of the people and at the expense of democracy.

Remember also, the EU approved the "extraordinary rendition" black box flights of the CIA, allowing the world's leading goon squad to scoop up anyone off the street, in silence, and sweep them away to a nice comfortable cell in Abu Ghraib, or some other "interrogation" centre. The EU has shown its commitment to corporate fascism, just as the American government has – only more discreetly, and slightly less brazenly. But let's stick to arguments that deal with economics and democratic independence for the moment, and set aside the gulag imagery which by now must also be associated with the EU, as with North America, in any honest discussion.

Iceland and Argentina show vastly better examples of a way forward than do Greece or Italy, even if they have their own struggles to contend with: tell the IMF to get stuffed, and say no to neo-liberalism and corporate hegemony. Go independent, renew democracy, do the exact opposite of what the IMF "recommends", and align intelligently with countries that wish for democracy, freedom, justice, peace, and mutual aid through trade and peaceful solidarity. This is the outline of a path ahead for countries that do not wish to follow the herd down well-trodden corridors, into the valley of steel, but instead wish for sanity, justice, authentic democracy and well-being for all.

The BRICs are rising, the EU and North America sinking: even economically, it is better to be outside of these blocs of decaying empire than in. Go with the BRIC alliance economically and MERCOSUR, and ditch the sinking ship, I would say to Scotland, Ireland, Greece and Spain, and other countries of a more independent spirit than is the present norm. My advice for Canada is the same, but people here are a wee bit deef. (That's deef with two e's.)

But this is what I most wanted to convey, and to hear your thoughts on (so I said to my friend, and so I say now to you, dear reader).

The three kayas, or spheres, of human society: Consciousness, culture, social structures and renaissance.

We have the dynamics of power inverted in our minds – and this is the reason for the slowness of social change, which is unfolding, from below, from the grassroots, from the people, despite such obstacles. We tend to unconsciously envision a pyramid structure of power in the world: and this part of our thinking is largely correct – power is concentrated at the top, and flows downward, to we plebes and cogs and consumers below. But this merely reflects the surface dynamics of power however – from above to below.

The pyramid of actual power, and not merely superficial, derivative power, has its peak below, in human consciousness, which in turn expresses itself in culture above it, and finally emerges as the social structures, systems and institutions which form the outward physical attributes of our society. We are mistaking skin for brain, and are mistaking effect with cause.

The causal relations work both ways of course: both up and down – from material conditions and social structures of power, which are above, to culture and consciousness which are below; and also from consciousness and culture below, to social institutions and structures of power above. But it is the bottom, the foundation, which holds all the real power, and not the top.

To view things from an overly superficial outlook is disastrous, for it impales us on a spear of falsely perceived powerlessness and dependency, from which we seek to escape, but upon which we will forever squirm, so long as we retain in our minds the illusion of externally-seated power.

It is imperative, if we wish for freedom, for justice, for democracy, for ecological sanity, for peace, or for a decent future for ourselves, our children, our grandchildren, or for any life on earth, that we now overcome our illusions with regards to the nature and dynamics of power. This is the heart of the matter. All else is secondary. If we grasp this, then we are on our way to a renaissance. If we fail to grasp this, then it is indeed, a dark age ahead. This is the crux, and the pivotal question.

But this is a just a short synopsis of what I am attempting to convey here, and what I believe is vital for us now to understand. Below is a brief elaboration of the view of where real power lies in any human society. I hope you will find it thought-provoking, if not liberating, and an inspiring call to action, and to the best in us all.

I really like the three-fold view of society that has come to my mind, and that I've thought about a lot over the past decade or so. In short, it is this. Body, speech and mind are the symbolic representations of the three principle spheres of human society, which in reverse order indicate consciousness, culture and social structures.

The body of society is its outward physical form: the structures of society we live with – economic, political and other social institutions, systems and structures of power. The speech of society is its culture, which is the dance or flux of the expressions of its thoughts. Mind is mind – the foundation and birth place of all that is. We are the creators of our reality, and pretending we are not only leads to misery as well as to passivity in the face of evil.

All three bodies or spheres of society – consciousness, culture and social structures – are both causes and effects: none is independent or separate from the rest; all three are interdependent as well as interpenetrating. Consciousness, culture and social structures: each effect the other two. By addressing any one of the three, all three are influenced.

The macrocosm of society is the reflection of the microcosm of the individual, just as the microcosm of the individual is the reflection of the macrocosm of the universe. As above, so below. The Renaissance thinkers knew, or redis-covered this basic principle of life, and we should now rediscover it ourselves, if we want a renaissance, or, by this time, any future at all.

The universe, the individual and the society could also be viewed as three interpenetrating and interdependent spheres. From the ground of being, which we may call the cosmos among other names, arises the expression of the ground of being, which is the individual being. From the interaction and collective voices, acts and expressions of individuals, arises what we label as society. All three are empty of inherent existence, all three are in eternal flux, and all three are interpenetrating and interdependent.

With the microcosm of the individual, body speech and mind – or we could call it, body, spirit and mind, or body, energy and mind – are three interpen-etrating and interdependent spheres, each one influencing and affecting the other two. We should naturally take care of all three. Nevertheless, it is mind, and not body, which is primary, and the prime mover or fundamental causal power. Our materialist reductionism has brought us much knowledge, but has eclipsed our view of the whole, the depths, the fundamental, the foun-dations, and hence, we see even the parts through a cloud of superstition presumption and confused misunderstanding.

Our shallow, flat-lander materialist bias also skews, distorts and clouds our understanding of our society and world, and if this is not corrected, we will in all likelihood destroy ourselves. All three spheres of society – consciousness, culture and social structures – as we have said, are interdependent, and each one is a major centre of power or causal influence. Therefore, we should naturally address and take care of all three. Yet, whatever we may choose as our focus, it is important for us to understand the nature of the relationship between these three interpenetrating and interdependent spheres of society, and the causal relations or power dynamics between and among them. If we do not, then we will understand very little, and as a result, we are likely to accomplish little, despite even herculean efforts.

Understanding is critical. Clarity is the first order of the day – today, and every day. From clarity and compassion, combined with courage, all good things come. Without clarity, we are lost, and a good heart or brave soul will amount to little in terms of real results.

A couple of notes must be made here, so that no misunderstanding is made. As there is no actual thing or being which is society – the Hobbesian imaginings of Leviathan being rather a dangerous and delusional concept – society is a gathering of individuals. This is essential to bear in mind. Sacrificing the individual to an imaginary greater whole is dangerous, and also the basis of all tyrannies.

Individuals are diverse; hence, the thoughts or expressions of mind which make up a culture are also diverse. Human beings are always in flux, as all things are, hence culture is also always in flux. The ebbs and flows, waves and motions of a culture are like wind in wheat fields, or rain on a still lake, or moonlight on a rippling river. Mind is the river, the ocean. Culture and thought are the waves on the surface.

However diverse, the expressions of human consciousness on a collective scale are precisely the definition and the fact of human culture. And just as consciousness is a power of greatly underestimated capacities, so too is culture a force of massively underestimated power. When culture moves gently, it is the waves which steadily lap at the sand castles of our social institutions, which seem, deceptively, so permanent and unchangeable. When culture moves forcefully, it is a tsunami, and it is irresistible – no reactionary force can stand in its way.

The mind of society is the collective consciousness or noosphere of all individuals: It is the interdependence and interaction of millions and billions of beings, and the consciousness of each shapes the collective gestalt or predominant patterns of thinking and views.

It would be easy to view oneself as lost in a sea and therefore powerless, since we are but a single drop in a great ocean, or one single voice in a great chorus, one instrument in a great symphony; but we are never powerless, for all beings and things are forever intertwined and interdependent. *If you are breathing, you have power.*

We are each sharing in the collective creation of our reality, day by day, and moment by moment. If you want to play powerless, go ahead, but it is an illusion, and it is playing dead. Worst of all, you cannot play dead without in some degree becoming the living dead. Choose to live while you live. Embrace your power.

Within the three kayas, (yes, the term is borrowed from Buddhism), the three bodies, spheres or aspects of human society, which are (physical) body, speech and mind – as with the human individual, mind is most powerful and most fundamental. Yes, material conditions, physical and social environment, economic, political and cultural structures and patterns do shape individual human consciousness – clearly so, and powerfully so. But human beings are *determined* by their environment rather than being the masters of their own minds, only when they allow themselves to be reduced to machines, and when the locus of power has been shifted *by the individual* from internal to external: meaning, *we are powerless only when we have succumbed to the illusion of powerlessness.*

Marx was wrong. Mind shapes matter far more powerfully than matter shapes mind. The two are interactive and interdependent, and mind, if it is self-aware, has the greater power. If we yield our power to outer material conditions, and say that we are a victim of circumstance, that is our choice, and our delusion. This may seem harsh, but an ideology of powerlessness is self-evisceration, and must be shunned and rejected completely and categorically. There is no blame here, only an embrace of our power. Of course, compassion and patience for both ourselves and others is necessary and intelligent. But the true nature of mind and matter remains, and must be dealt with, if we are to deal in the real world, and not solely relate to the mere projections of our minds.

Hegel should have turned Marx on his head; instead, he is turning in his grave. Marx was an extremely lucid sociologist, albeit a poor political philosopher and a terrible political strategist, but despite his often lucid thought, his materialist bias remains a major, glaring weakness. While Hegel was an even worse political philosopher, being a starry-eyed and delusional statist, he did come closer to the truth than did Marx when it comes to pure philosophy – especially ontology, or the study of the nature of being. Mind is more primary than body or matter – or spirit, as Hegel preferred to call it – and not the other way around, as Marx believed.

Matter is the weaker party in the mutually-arising interdependence of the two primary polarities of existence, the binary code of life, which are mind and matter, or more precisely, consciousness and form. This means also that both environment and conditioning are less powerful than mind, and can be overcome or transformed. To miss this, is to render yourself, along with others, a slave and a pawn and a mere reactionary, a leaf in the wind, a lump of clay. *To recognize the power of mind, the power of the human spirit, is to realize that all things are transmutable, and we are the makers of our destiny.*

In sociological or political terms, what this means is that we are re-creating our world every day. We can re-create and reproduce the same old patterns – patterns of war and greed, fear and hate, empire and injustice and suicidal tendencies, ad nauseum, ad infinitum, or at least until we drive ourselves into extinction, *if we choose* – or if we drift along in a stupor of quiet desperation or habitual passivity, and choose by default, by letting the power hungry choose for us, as they most certainly will. Or, as Thomas Paine said, we can realize that it is in our power to create the world anew. *It is our power, and it is our choice whether we will embrace our power, or deny it. The future hangs upon that decision. As Einstein said, the world is a dangerous place, not because of the terrible things done by a few, but because the many allow such terrible things to be committed. Denial of our power is thus at the heart of all social and ecological problems. This must be overcome, to say it mildly.*

Consciousness is the foundation of human society, and the most powerful causal element in historical flux or change, and in the shaping of both our individual and collective realities. From mind arises speech, or the expressions of mind. This, on the collective level of human interaction, is culture. From mind and culture arise the day to day creation or re-creation (the perpetuation) of social structures, which forms the outward physical form or body of society.

The body of society is the visible outward forms of our culture and consciousness, as expressed in the social institutions, power structures and systems which sanctify, sometimes deify, calcify, reify and reproduce the power dynamics and views which are the outgrowth of our assumptions, beliefs, consciousness and values.

Of course, there is a large gap between the social institutions on the one hand, and the culture and consciousness of the people on the other, and that is because the elite tend historically and also presently to dominate the social structures and institutions, and the people's views and values are divergent and largely silenced and suppressed. *The gap or divergence* between culture and consciousness, that is, the people, on the one hand, and on the other hand, the outward structures of power, *can only hold so long as the people remain sufficiently passive, and do not exert, embrace or even acknowledge their power.* When the people do begin to embrace their power, as is beginning to happen now, the social structures and institutions are forced to come in line with the views and values of the people. This is what is called a revolution. And this is precisely what is needed, and is emerging now, from beneath the rubble of the crumbling weight of a dying order.

When the structures and institutions of a society come into conflict with the trajectory or currents of culture and human consciousness, the seemingly immovable, yet brittle and merely superficial power of those structures and institutions begin rapidly to lose their mesmerizing power, and to crumble and dissolve: it is social structures which yield to culture, in the long run, and not the other way around.

In short, the people have the power, whether they realize it or not – the outward power structures are merely derivative, and thus also, ever tentative, amendable, and open to revision, revolution, or simply being cast off, in favour of new and more useful forms of human interaction. This is what is happening now.

Structure is a blind edifice. Culture is the life blood of society. Culture trumps structure, sooner or later, if ever there is a conflict between the two. Social structures and institutions shape culture and consciousness, naturally, and powerfully so, but consciousness and culture are more fundamental and more powerful than mere social structures, and when consciousness and culture shift, structures and systems and institutions are forced to change. *There may be a battle, but consciousness and culture always trump mere outward social structures in the end, and periodically, they do so with ferocious speed.*

Culture shifts when mind shifts. When there is a shift in consciousness, attitudes or views, then the culture by necessity begins to shift; and when the culture begins to shift, by necessity, the structures of society are dragged along and compelled to change – or are cast aside.

Social structures, power structures, systems and institutions are resistant to change, and may have to be made to come along kicking and screaming, to bend to the will of the people; but in any event, peacefully or with a temper tantrum, they are forced to change when consciousness and culture changes, and cannot resist for long.

When a major cultural shift is unfolding, and that shift is toward a greater openness and clarity of thought and consciousness, then a renaissance is at hand – and the political, economic and other social institutions and structures of power had better embrace the flux, or be prepared to be swept into the dust bin of history, along with all the irrelevancy of an order whose time has passed.

We are at such a juncture in history now. Be prepared for an exciting ride. It's not over yet, and the ride may yet be quite rough, but the outcome will be good. And for those who despair and scoff, and say that no such renaissance could possibly be unfolding amidst this mess, I would say with Yogi Berra: "It ain't over till it's over."

There is more day yet to dawn.

JTR
February 13, 2012

"ZBIG" BRZEZINSKI:
ELITE PLANNING FOR GLOBAL EMPIRE

ZBIGNIEW BRZENISKI, A LEADING architect of corporate-driven globalization and the present global corporate empire under which we live, believes, quite frankly, as he has said explicitly, that democracy is an obstacle to both elite rule and global empire, and therefore should be dismantled. He also believes that the era of the nation-state is obsolete, and national democracies should be folded into a global government run by the world's business elite and a handful of self-proclaimed intellectual demigods such as himself. (The World Economic Forum, IMF, World Bank and WTO, along with a few other transnational organizations and rich men's clubs, represent the "de facto world government" that has been created for these purposes.) The general consensus among the international business and political elite is in agreement with Brzezinski on these two points, as their private statements, and even more so, their continued actions, have made perfectly clear. It would be wise for us to understand what the presently ruling elite have in mind and are driving towards. Otherwise, we will be unable to effectively defend democracy and freedom, or work for a world based in justice, ecological sanity and peace. For that reason, the writings of elite planners like Zbig, along with NSC68, PNAC and Trilateral Commission publications, and other extremely influential and revealing documents, are important for us to look at. Mistaking public rhetoric for actual intentions is highly unwise, to say the least. We should know what we're dealing with.

❧

The phrase "technotronic era," from the title of one of Brzezinski's earlier books from 1969, *Between Two Ages: America's Role in the New Technotronic Era*, may sound strange to us. The phrase may sound so odd that we may even be inclined to think this is an irrelevant book by some wing-nut or flake from the periphery who doesn't really know what's going on, since he speaks in such strange language and can't even speak properly. This would be a mistake.

"Zbig," as he likes to be called, is the chief long-term geostrategic planner for the Western political and business elite, and has been so ever since he superseded Kissinger in that role in the mid-1970's. He was co-founder of the Trilateral Commission – the 300 member elite think tank and planning group created in 1973, which stacked the U.S. government with its members during the Carter administration, and has been tightly wedded to elite U.S. political power as well as the business and political elite of North America, Europe and Japan (hence the name trilateral) ever since. He was appointed by President Obama as his National Security Advisor, and has been the leading intellectual in residence for the Western elite for nearly four decades.

The phrase "technotronic era" does sound strange to us, but that is only because it did not catch on and become popularized, or become part of our familiar lexicon. Instead we use phrases like "digital revolution" or "technocratic" to describe what he was talking about. But his phrase is perfectly apt as well. In his book he was talking about the goal of global domination, elite rule and control of the population through technological and other means. He was advocating a kind of Orwellian big brother society on a global scale. It may be hard to believe, but some people actually like that sort of thing, especially if they hope to be among the ruling elite. Maybe Zbigniew is a very nice guy with his family and friends, but in terms of human society, his views and agenda are positively ghoulish.

> *"The technotronic era involves the gradual appearance of a more controlled society. Such a society would be dominated by an elite,*

unrestrained by traditional values. Soon it will be possible to assert almost continuous surveillance over every citizen and maintain up-to-date complete files containing even the most personal information about the citizen. These files will be subject to instantaneous retrieval by the authorities. "

– *Zbigniew Brzezinski,* Between Two Ages: America's Role in the Technotronic Era

And remember, Brzezinski is among the *liberal* wing of the ruling elite. The neo-conservatives are even further off the chart in terms of imperial madness and self-justifying delusions of grandeur. The neo-liberals are simply bloodless, vampiric, elitist technocrats, hell-bent on dominating the world and making themselves into the new pharaohs. The neo-cons are exactly the same, with the same agenda, except that they believe they're on a mission from God. We've come a long way since the time of Jefferson and Thomas Paine. The world is a dangerous place, and the greatest danger is from our own self-proclaimed "leaders." God save us from such diabolical "saviours of humanity."

"Zbig" knows very well what is going on in the world: he just happens to be on the side of the ruling elite, and not the people, and is in favour of a one-world government run by the corporate and financial elite and a few intellectuals, such as himself, who serve them – as he has made explicit in his writings and speeches. He is rabidly anti-democratic, and believes in a global elite rule. He is the modern day Machiavelli – except that Machiavelli only dared dream of being the favoured advisor to a prince who ruled a city-state; Brzezinski has his eyes on a global empire. His views may disgust us, and should, but he certainly has a pretty clear understanding of what is going on. We can in fact look to him, along with certain others, to see just what the business and political elite have in mind – and we should. Know your enemy.

Below are a few quotes to consider. And remember who this guy is, what team he plays for, and what his level is in that team: he is at the top in terms of long-term planning for the elite, even if he is only an employee or courtesan for the presently ruling elite business class.

We should also note that while most intellectuals unconsciously or consciously serve a propaganda function for the ruling elite, and address as their audience the masses who are supposed to be indoctrinated, deceived, fed "necessary illusions" and other fanciful tales in order to manufacture consent and maintain public docility, Zbig does not work in that area. That is not his shtick. He writes for the elite, as a planner and analyst, and the general public are not supposed to pay attention to what he says. Thus, his writings tend to be more honest than those of someone like Samuel Huntington, or Thomas Friedman, whose writings are pure rubbish and fairy tale, as they very likely know – although, it is fairly common that propagandists believe their own lies, so it is hard to tell.

Most intellectuals are conscious, or more often unconscious, propagandists for the ruling class. Not Brezinski – he is a planner, strategist and advisor to the ruling class. He serves a different role for the masters, and hence writes and speaks in a different mode. Zbig writes as he sees it, for the benefit of the rulers, with a frankness that is chilling. He is an unapologetic elitist and imperialist, and makes no bones about his absolute opposition to democracy, or to what he calls "traditional values," meaning, human sympathy, compassion, or any moral standards other than the pursuit and maintenance of power.

Brzezinski does seem to believe that America's global hegemony is the safeguard for global security, and the world is a safer place because of the American empire, but that is not surprising. Every emperor, or loyal servant of the emperor, has believed that the world is a better place because of their heroic and selfless actions. Such delusions are common among sociopaths and the power-hungry. Hitler, Stalin, Mussolini and Mao all thought they were making the world a better place. "The vile maxim of the masters," as Adam Smith called it, has always been, as Smith described it so cogently and honestly, "all for us, nothing for anybody else." But of course, the self-proclaimed "masters of the universe," as the current power elite now call themselves, rationalize and justify their greed and hubris, as their predecessors have always done. So Zbig lies to himself, too – what can you expect? He does spell out the plans and goals of the Western elite quite candidly however, and that is why we should be interested in what he has to say.

"And those that possess, steal from the ones without possessions
The message I stress: to make it stop study your lessons
Don't settle for less...
The power is in the people"

– Tupac

"All men are caught in an escapable network of mutuality."

– Martin Luther King Jr.

"A nation or civilization that continues to produce soft-minded men
purchases its own spiritual death on an instalment plan."

– Martin Luther King Jr.

If we want to know what are the motivations and goals of the elite – and we had better know and understand them – we should look at the record of their actions, most essentially, and not just their rhetoric; and we should also look at their own private statements, which are meant to be heard or read only within elite circles, and which the public is not supposed to hear, read or pay attention to, but which are often readily available, if we want to look at them.

From *The Grand Chessboard*, 1997

"The last decade of the twentieth century has witnessed a tectonic shift in
world affairs. For the first time ever, a non-Eurasian power has emerged
not only as a key arbiter of Eurasian power relations but also as the
world's paramount power. The defeat and collapse of the Soviet Union
was the final step in the rapid ascendance of a Western Hemisphere
power, the United States, as the sole and, indeed, the first truly global
power." (p. xiii)

"Ever since the continents started interacting politically,
some five hundred years ago, Eurasia has been the center
of world power."- (p. xiii)

"It is imperative that no Eurasian challenger emerges capable
of dominating Eurasia and thus of also challenging America.

The formulation of a comprehensive and integrated Eurasian geostrategy is therefore the purpose of this book." (p. xiv)

"How America 'manages' Eurasia is critical. A power that dominates Eurasia would control two of the world's three most advanced and economically productive regions. A mere glance at the map also suggests that control over Eurasia would almost automatically entail Africa's subordination, rendering the Western Hemisphere and Oceania geopolitically peripheral to the world's central continent. About 75 per cent of the world's people live in Eurasia, and most of the world's physical wealth is there as well, both in its enterprises and underneath its soil. Eurasia accounts for about three-fourths of the world's known energy resources." (p.31)

"Never before has a populist democracy attained international supremacy. But the pursuit of power is not a goal that commands popular passion, except in conditions of a sudden threat or challenge to the public's sense of domestic well-being. The economic self-denial (that is, defense spending) and the human sacrifice (casualties, even among professional soldiers) required in the effort are uncongenial to democratic instincts. Democracy is inimical to imperial mobilization." (p.35)

"To put it in a terminology that harkens back to the more brutal age of ancient empires, the three grand imperatives of imperial geostrategy are to prevent collusion and maintain security dependence among the vassals, to keep tributaries pliant and protected, and to keep the barbarians from coming together." (p.40)

"The momentum of Asia's economic development is already generating massive pressures for the exploration and exploitation of new sources of energy and the Central Asian region and the Caspian Sea basin are known to contain reserves of natural gas and oil that dwarf those of Kuwait, the Gulf of Mexico, or the North Sea."(p.125)

"In the long run, global politics are bound to become increasingly uncongenial to the concentration of hegemonic power in the hands of a single state. Hence, America is not only the first, as well as the only, truly global superpower, but it is also likely to be the very last." (p.209)

"Moreover, as America becomes an increasingly multi-cultural society, it may find it more difficult to fashion a consensus on foreign policy issues, except in the circumstance of a truly massive and widely perceived direct external threat."(p. 211)*

Brzezinski lamenting the global awakening of humanity:

"For the first time in human history almost all of humanity is politically activated, politically conscious and politically interactive... The resulting global political activism is generating a surge in the quest for personal dignity, cultural respect and economic opportunity in a world painfully scarred by memories of centuries-long alien colonial or imperial domination... [The] major world powers, new and old, also face a novel reality: while the lethality of their military might be greater than ever, their capacity to impose control over the politically awakened masses of the world is at a historic low. To put it bluntly: in earlier times, it was easier to control one million people than to physically kill one million people; today, it is infinitely easier to kill one million people than to control one million people."*

- Zbigniew Brzezinski, speaking to the CFR in Montreal, spring 2010

Most important is to know thyself, which means knowing your dignity, your basic goodness and your power, above all. The second most important thing is to know your opponent. If you believe in democracy, freedom, justice, peace, ecological sanity, or a decent life and future for all, then you should realize that the currently ruling elite are opponents, in practice if not in rhetoric, to all of these values and goals. Know yourself. Know your enemy. Peace will win, but only if practiced with boldness and awareness.

JTR
February 18, 2012

THE STATE OF THE WORLD

"We're writing the history of the future...

The people who are going to survive and thrive are the ones who are going to prepare

– the ones who are going to see history before it happens and get ready for it."

– Gerald Celente

(Note: This article was originally written in February, 2012. On June 1, 2012 the UN declared that we are at a tipping point, warning that the earth's environmental systems "are being pushed towards their biophysical limits" and that sudden, irreversible and potentially catastrophic changes are looming. There is no more denying that we are facing grave dangers.)

The world is full of beauty and goodness. It is also full of suffering and terrible things. Which side of the equation we foster and nourish, and which we avoid or minimize, is now up to us, as it always has been.

There are very hopeful, promising, positive trends unfolding in the world now; and there are very dark and menacing trends that are unfolding as well. To see the good is wise. To see the negative and the dangers is necessary, and also prudent.

As to the dangers, which this article will focus upon – other articles and essays have outlined some of the more positive trends – there are three that stand out above all. Barring the unthinkable, which is the madness of nuclear, chemical or biological warfare, or the cataclysmic effects of a large scale nuclear accident – all of which are still grave and present dangers – there are three major threats facing humanity now that rise above all others. These I wish to outline here, and also to outline what I believe to be a sensible, responsible and prudent response.

(Again, this is assuming that we can avoid nuclear or biochemical holocaust – which I trust and pray we will have the sanity to do. But if Obama and the other insane advocates of unending imperial war do decide to attack Iran, which has a military and economic alliance with two opposing nuclear super-powers – Russia and China – then anything can happen, and all our necks are strung out on the line. Prevent war with Iran at all costs. It is an utterly insane gambit for further global hegemony by a pack of greed-driven madmen, hell-bent on global domination. The Wall Street gang must be dethroned – they are risking not only all our lives, but the very future of humanity on Earth. See Chomsky, Chossudovsky and Celente on this issue, among others. This is also assuming that the Fukushima reactors are fixed in time, and that a cataclysmic nuclear accident is averted – which at the time of this writing, is certainly in question. Shout from the rooftops: fix Fukushima now – and ban all nukes! There is no such thing as safe nuclear power or nuclear weapons.)

Remember, the following is not prophecy – it is prediction. It is not even that: it is simply the mapping of our current trajectories, which if left unchanged, will take us exactly where we are heading. And it is not hard to see where we are heading. In fact, it takes great determination not to see it. The writing is on the wall.

It does not take a crystal ball to see what is going on, and what is rapidly unfolding. It simply takes a modest amount of honesty and courage to face the obvious. We would have to succumb to a possibly fatal and extraordinarily unwise wilful ignorance, a chosen or unconscious denial, in order to avoid facing the present realities which now stare us in the face. I am not saying these things will happen: I am saying they are possible, and by now, probable – that given our current trajectory, unless we change course, these things will hit us between the eyes, and soon. We had best address them now. Waiting to see what happens is the most dangerous thing we can do.

The three greatest near term dangers facing humanity:
(Barring nuclear or biochemical cataclysm, of course, which we must also work to prevent)

1. Economic depression and/or collapse – and the fallout and political repression that will likely also ensue from that

2. Fascism

3. Ecological cataclysm leading to social and civilizational collapse

The time-frame is most likely in that same order of unfolding:

1. Economic depression or collapse:

0 days to 2-4 years+

> *"What we believe...is that there's going to be some kind of geopolitical event – false flag or otherwise – that's going to spin the world's equity markets into a downward spiral that we've never seen before, and they're going to blame it on some kind of a terrorist or a geopolitical boogie man, while the underlying cause [laughs] is, clearly, an economic debacle that has been foisted upon us by the Federal Reserve and the central banks world-wide by pumping worthless fiat money into the systems to keep the ponzi scheme going. And people forget, it's not only the Fed, or the ECB that's been doing it – China's been doing it since 2008, when they pumped in over 4.5 trillion Yuen into pumping up their system. It's all one big bubble, and it's ready to burst. It's only a question of how long can they keep getting away with this....*
>
> *Those who aren't prepared will lose everything...*
>
> *If you follow the leaders you're going to fail. We're going into the Greatest Depression. It's going to be worse than the '29 depression....*

In the '30's we had trade surpluses and balanced budgets; we had budget surpluses, not $10.5 trillion in the hole; we had a manufacturing base to produce our way out of this...

And when I look at people looking to Washington to solve the problem – I'm an open-minded man, I'm a trends researcher, I look at data, and information – show me one, one program that they can say, "Look at the great job that we did." Oh, Katrina, great job...

They used to say, we agree with you, but can't you say something positive?

Ya, like, the ship is going down, but doesn't the band sound great?

But people are afraid of the truth."

– Gerald Celente, Trends Research

The currency crisis that is almost certain to explode at some point in the near future will in all likelihood trigger a severe global economic depression. When the greater depression hits, it will be global, since all of the world's central banks are holding U.S. currency, the world's de facto reserve currency, and the U.S. currency is certain to collapse, for the reasons outlined above (pumping out fiat currency at break-neck speed, which massively devalues the currency), as well as for reasons of severe and long-standing trade deficits. You can't produce nothing, and keep getting paid for it, which is what has been happening. And you can't keep printing money out of thin air without radically devaluing and destabilizing the currency, which is also what has been happening. Sooner or later the bubble bursts, and that time is rapidly approaching, as the best and most honest economists and commentators have warned. (See Max Keiser for honest and intelligent, in-depth financial reporting and analysis.)

We already have millions of homeless people in the Western world. There are half a million homeless children in the United States alone. People are losing their homes daily. Foreclosure rates are through the roof. Personal and business bankruptcy rates are through the roof (while those at the top grow ever more staggeringly rich). Millions of people are just one or two pay-cheques away from losing their homes – job loss would mean home loss, and most jobs are now precarious, with virtually no job security anywhere.

Twenty-something, thirty-something and older grown children are moving back home to live with their parents because they can't find anything other than Mcjobs. Personal debt in the U.S. now exceeds the national debt. In Canada, people are spending on average 180% of their income, meaning they are rapidly sinking deeper and deeper into debt. Baby boomers and virtually all others – aside from the richest 1% – are swamped with debt, and are feeling the ground dropping away beneath them as they struggle to stay afloat. And after a lifetime of struggle and hard work, the majority of people now will retire into poverty, if they can retire at all.

To put it succinctly, the great majority of people are already having a very hard time. What will happen when the central banks of Europe, China, Japan and Saudi Arabia all simultaneously dump their U.S. currency reserves, which they are definitely going to do, with each group holding roughly a trillion dollars of hyper-devalued, worthless U.S. currency? World-wide, currencies will crash in cascading, rapid succession, with only a few nations faring the storm relatively well – mainly the BRIC nations, and those that have wisely decoupled from the U.S. dollar and diversified trade away from North America and Europe. (Mecosur for example, will likely fare better than most regions.) In short, the bottom will fall out of the global economy, and the proverbial shit will hit the fan.

When and if a depression hits – and it is highly likely, if not certain that it will – the remainder of the vanishing middle class will be wiped out, and will join the growing ranks of the poor and the underclass, while poverty skyrockets. Considering the deep discontent and frustrations of the people already, as witnessed, for example, by the riots in Greece and Spain, depression may very well mean riots in the streets in virtually every major city. It will mean that revolution explodes.

As Gerald Celente says, "When people lose everything, and they have nothing left to lose, they lose it." What depression would also likely mean, is revolution in the streets, as Celente also predicts.

(Note that Gerald Celente's track record of predictions is stunning, including the prediction of the collapse of the Soviet Union, when virtually no one was predicting it, the market crash of '87, the Asian financial tsunami, the dot com bubble collapse, the housing bubble collapse, the recession that started in 2007, and a string of other successful, startlingly accurate predictions. CNN calls him the best in the business of tracking and predicting trends, and he is relied upon by all the major media, as well as large corporations and governments for his extremely accurate trend predictions. The *New York Times* has said, "If Nostradamus were alive today, he would have a hard time competing with Gerald Celente.")

> *"When the money stops flowing down to the street,*
> *blood will flow in the streets."*
>
> *– Gerald Celente*

The rise of revolution will be non-violent in the main, but in times of severe economic crisis, with tensions high, you can be assured that some few at least will turn violent. And of course, what happens then? Between riots and revolution, legitimate or otherwise, governments will bring in the heavy hand to enforce "order." The harder the economic crash, the bigger the upheaval, the greater the iron fist in response.

Prepare for an economic tsunami, and also, for the even worse repercussions that will follow. Prepare now for difficult economic times, and even more importantly, stand up for liberty and democracy now, before the jack boot comes down – before dissent and freedom of speech are not only criminalized, but forcibly suppressed. If you value your freedom, speak up now.

2. Fascism:

Fascism is here now – it is only a question of when the heavy handed repression comes, and the round-up of dissidents and their families begins in earnest. One more terrorist attack, real or staged, or war with Iran, or the fast-approaching economic collapse, will be enough to unleash the hounds, and the gloves will really come off. I have written extensively on this clear and present danger, and documented the evidence with what should be overwhelming demonstration of the threat. For the moment, we will leave the topic aside, and turn to the third great risk. For the benefit of any who still have doubts, we will return to the subject later.

3. Ecological cataclysm leading to social and civilizational collapse:

Timeline: unpredictable.

All we can say is that it is virtually certain within 100 years, and quite possibly within 10 to 20, unless radical changes are made very soon, that our civilization will collapse under the weight of an ecological cataclysm of our own making. Prudence would prescribe preparation.

"How soon till we drop off that cliff ahead, Fred?"

" I dunno Barney – let's keep driving."

"Ok Fred."

Apathy, denial, paralysis or business-as-usual are not sane responses to the crisis we face. We should prepare now for a possible crash, as well as turning the wheel and hitting the brakes, or we will drive ourselves back into the Stone Age, if not into extinction.

We do not understand nearly enough the complex ecology of the planet and how we are changing it, to say that a collapse of our civilization due to the strains of severe ecological disaster will not happen within the next five to 10 years, or even the next one to two years. It *appears* that it will take at least another five to 10 years, and more likely 10 to 20 or more of gradual increase in the frequency and severity of ecological disasters before the strain could be expected to potentially break down our infrastructure and hence our civilization. *But,* this is if we experience only a linear and gradual increase, and have no sudden major changes. And what we now know from systems theory, ecology, chaos theory and Illya Prigogine's work, is that sudden radical changes can and do happen. We would be extremely unwise to assume that gradual, linear progressions of trends are the only possibility. Nature also has punctuation marks.

We know that unless we change course, sudden major changes are definitely coming; and they are difficult to predict as to when they will occur; and that they will be triggered by events we have already put into motion – such as the melting of the permafrost, the reversal of major ocean currents such as the Gulf Stream, and the burning of the rainforests, all caused by the cumulative effects of anthropogenic global warming. Each of these, when they happen, if we allow them to happen, or if we cannot avert them in time, will unleash disaster on this world of truly apocalyptic proportions. Humanity will survive, but this civilization most certainly would not. It would collapse like a house of cards, as other civilizations have done before.

But for the moment, let us leave aside the unknown variables of sudden radical shifts in ecology which could precipitate a collapse of our infrastructure and civilization. They must be considered and planned for, and averted wherever possible, but for the moment, let us leave them aside. Let us look simply at the cumulative effects of steadily mounting ecological disasters, which have been increasing in severity and frequency for some decades now.

When Hurricane Katrina hit, the results were of course devastating. Part of the blame lies with a government that did not care – either before or after the event. Preparation for the predicted event was shunned, and disaster response was slow and severely lacking. What is also true is that the frequency and severity of storms has been increasing exponentially for more than two decades – due to the pernicious effects of the tooth fairy (that other boogie man being a complete ruse, of course).

An even more important fact to consider is that in the two months before and after Katrina, at least five other major ecological disasters struck the world. With ecological disasters increasing in frequency and severity, and just a single one of them, Katrina, able to swamp our response efforts, it is not hard to predict a time in the not too distant future when disasters hit with such force, so close together, one after the other, that our infrastructure and entire civilization begins to crumble under the strain. Whether the breakdown and collapse of infrastructure and civilization comes in 100 years, or 50, 20, 10, or less, is entirely uncertain. Prudence would dictate preparedness. You don't expect to have a car accident when you get into a car, but you buckle your seat belt anyway, just in case. Prudence here is basic sanity, if not clarity of prescience. It is also a matter of responsibility to our fellow human beings – particularly the children of the world. If we are most bold, brave and successful, we will avert the collapse of human civilization, by making the necessary changes swiftly and decisively. If we are not so courageous or brave, then we had best be prepared for the worst – for all of our courage will be needed to deal with the unfortunate results of our inaction.

But this is just looking at the gradual increase in cumulative effects from mounting ecological disasters. We now should return to look at just a few ways that sudden changes could bring down our entire civilization. This is not morbidity by the way – this is preparing for the worst in order to foster the best. It is sensible prudence to look toward the future, if not for our own sake, then for the ones we love, and for all living beings on this small and beautiful, fragile planet.

When the tsunami hit South East Asia in 2004, the devastation was extreme. The cause was an undersea earthquake, and it was accounted for as a natural disaster. The fact is that seismic activity has been increasing over the past few decades, for reasons that are poorly understood. (Watch for Yosemite. Watch Fukushima as well.)

Another important fact to consider is that such a tsunami or others like it, or even more severe, can also be caused, and will likely be caused, when very large parts of the Antarctic Ice Sheet break off and fall into the ocean. The Ice Sheet is melting, and when, not if the West Antarctic Ice Sheet falls, it will cause a tsunami that will dwarf that of 2004, rising hundreds of feet above sea level; and it will hit most coastlines in the world within nine hours. Sixty percent of the major population centres of the world are within five metres of sea level. Most of the world's financial and manufacturing centres are also within five meters of sea level. And much of the world's agricultural production is within the danger zone as well. Such an event would certainly strain human civilization near if not past the breaking point. Denial says it won't happen in our lifetime, but denial is a fool's game. Global warming is unquestionably real, and the Ice Sheet will fall, sooner or later. The best scientific evidence suggests it could be within two decades.

If we allow global warming to continue unchecked, as we are doing now, the rain forests of the Amazon basin will also burn. This would cause such enormous clouds of smoke that agriculture globally would be seriously if not severely affected, and a global famine would ensue. The melting of the permafrost, due to global warming, would trigger even greater cataclysmic effects. The reversal of the Gulf Stream, due to the melting of the polar caps by global warming, would also create radical climatic changes, leading to catastrophic results. (See the David Suzuki Foundation or George Monbiot, among others, for further information and analysis.)

The fact is, we have strained the earth's ecosystems to the breaking point, *and continue to do so,* and we can expect *from our own actions and inactions,* as a result, such a calamity that would be severe enough to bring down our entire civilization. It has happened before. Jared Diamond and Ronald Wright have documented and warned us of how civilizations have collapsed in the past. Will we make the needed changes in time to avoid this fate? We still may. We should certainly do everything in our power to avoid bringing a cataclysm upon our heads, of course. We should also make preparations, in case we do not make the needed changes quickly enough. This should, by now, be obvious to any who are still capable of rational thought. I know the mass media, the politicians and the spin doctors are working hard to destroy any such capacity within the human mind, but certainly there are many who are not yet functionally brain dead, or lost in a paralysing miasma of quiet despair.

There may be other major ecological shifts that are coming, some of which we are aware, others not, and which could strike anytime, and be complete game-changers. An eruption of the volcanic lake under Yosemite, which would be the eruption of a super-volcano, would send up an ash cloud large enough to blot out the sun world wide for six years, radically cooling the planet and sending the Earth into an ice age, causing crop failure and starvation world-wide. Imagine what would happen if humanity couldn't grow anything for six years. Presently, the world has less than 30-40 days of food stocks globally. We have nowhere near the food stocks needed to last six years without a growing season. (Wildlife would perish with the volcanic winter as well, making hunting non-viable, unless we want to eat rats.) With an eruption of Yosemite, we would see the onset of a volcanic winter, and we would witness mass starvation across the globe. Scientists estimate over 60% of human life on earth would be wiped out. Industry, economies and infrastructure would slowly collapse due to severe labour shortages combined with loss of power and communication systems, with cascading results.

Civilization would teeter on the brink, or simply collapse. And Yosemite has been rumbling lately. Recently there have been magma-flow-induced earthquakes lasting weeks on end, which plate shift quakes do not exhibit. In 2000 the Bush administration is reported to have put a gag order on the U.S. Geological Service, forbidding it from speaking to the public regarding Yellowstone's super-volcano activity. Yosemite's underground magma pool is 70 kilometres long, 30 kilometres wide and 10 kilometres deep, and its eruption would be the equivalent of thousands of ordinary volcanoes erupting at once – more powerful than 60 million atom bombs. 300 million people live within the blast radius, but the effects would be global. One of the several super-volcano eruptions known to have occurred in the Earth's history is thought to have contributed to the extinction of the Neanderthal, 40,000 years ago. The Yosemite super-volcano, the largest known super-volcano on Earth, is known to go off approximately once every 600,000 years – and the last eruption was 640,000 years ago. Geological surveys show the Earth's crust is rising between half an inch to an inch a year over Yosemite, indicating the massive magma pool is being filled and pushing upward. Seismic activity confirms that the magma is building and the caldera, or volcanic crater, is becoming unstable. Yosemite is a level 8 super-volcano: VEI or Volcanic Explosivity Index 8. Such eruptions eject over 1,000 square kilometres of rock mass equivalent in the form of ash into the atmosphere, and are capable of being extinction level events. Certainly, they are cataclysmic. Again, humanity would survive – with difficulty – but civilization as we know it, in all likelihood would not. (See Michael Rampino, NYU volcanologist.)

Beyond the direct evidence that Yosemite may erupt sometime soon, there is another reason to be concerned. Astrophysicists now know that our solar system oscillates up and down in a cyclic motion above and below the galactic plane of our galaxy, also known as the galactic equinox or the dark rift. The galactic plane is the plane of maximum gravitational force exerted by the giant black hole at the centre of our galaxy, which has an estimated mass of a trillion suns. When our planet and solar system pass through that plane, which we are about to do, the gravitational force exerted on the earth and sun will cause major effects. On earth, seismic and volcanic activity will increase, among other effects. On the sun, solar flare and CME activity will increase. The result is that either an eruption of a super-volcano such as Yosemite, or a major hit by a large CME, becomes a much greater possibility. The time of our crossing of the galactic plane may prove to be pivotal in our history, as others have said in the past.

A direct hit by a large CME (a coronal mass ejection caused by solar flares from the sun) would also bring down our civilization in short order – and the sun has been increasing its CME activity recently in dramatic ways. When we see the Northern or Southern lights, we are seeing the effects of solar storms and CME's on the Earth's electromagnetic field. A direct hit by a major coronal mass ejection would not be so pretty – in fact, it would be devastating. So far we have been lucky, and have not had a direct hit. Such an event, were one to come, would fry our civilization's information, communication and electrical power systems with a massive EMP (electromagnetic pulse) wave, knocking out modern civilization, likely in one blow. Cities in particular would become essentially uninhabitable without electricity. With no electricity, there is no refrigeration, no water, no sewage systems, and of course, no TV, cable, internet, phones or electric light, and no gas pumps.... things would get ugly, very fast. With no food, water or sanitation, starvation, crime and disease would become epidemic within a matter of months. People would be forced to flee the cities, usually on foot, as the roads would all be clogged. If it happens to be winter when the power grid goes down and stays down, many would perish from the cold in the exodus out of the cities in search of food or safety. If it is summer, many will perish due to hunger. Anyone with land within 100 kilometres of a major city would be swamped with refugees searching for food and shelter – a few of them bearing guns and bad tempers. We would be returned to small villages of subsistence farmers in less than a year, rebuilding our lives and starting the project of civilization all over, very nearly from scratch, and certainly, from a much more modest level.

Barring these unpredictable events, we can say that civilizational collapse due to ecological crisis is probably more than 20 years away, and possibly as far away as 50 or 70 years. (It is quite certain from all evidence that we will not last beyond another 60 to 70 years at our current pace of ecological destruction, unless we make major changes very soon.) But this seemingly distant date for the collapse of our civilization due to our own ecological ignorance, arrogance and neglect, is absolutely uncertain, for the reasons just mentioned – it may come far sooner. We simply do not know. It will come within the lifetimes of the youngest children alive today, unless we make a major shift now, but it may come within the next five years, or even the next year. Prudence, precaution and preparation would be wise.

Change course, and also prepare the life boats – hopefully we will miss that looming iceberg and the Titanic will stay afloat. It is unlikely, I believe, for the simple reason that we have been too slow and too stubbornly locked in denial as to the dangers for too long. And so, while continuing to work for major change in human society, we should also prepare for what comes after the collapse of industrial civilization, even while we work for a shift in that civilization. Humanity will continue. This *present* civilization very well may not. In any event, whatever happens, unless it is a nuclear holocaust, it will not be the end: there will be more to come – it will be an ending and also a new beginning. Therefore, it is prudent to prepare. It is wise to act, and not simply to drift. And as always, our actions or inaction matter greatly. What comes after this present order of civilization falls, is up to us – and I assure you, it will fall, and soon, one way or another, by human action, or by human inaction.

As Dylan said, "He who isn't busy being born is busy dying." Get busy living or get busy dying: we have no more time for mere drifting with inertia. It is time now to create, and to build.

It is time for us to accept that we are responsible for our collective destinies, and we must work together to prepare and to ensure our future, and that of our children and grandchildren. We should be real, above all: corporations are the major part of the problems we face, not the solution or the messiahs; and unless we have a major shift in government, and not simply a shift in faces, or the same faces, governments and corporations are NOT going to save us. Nor will science, technology or the church, by the way. All of these powers and institutions are potentially helpful, but presently, they are either too weak, too distracted, too lost in a la la land of denial, or too corrupted to be of much help. It is up to the people.

Do what you can to bring every major element and sphere and institution of human society into alignment with social and ecological needs – and do also keep in mind that it is up to us to save ourselves and one another. We the people must take responsibility for our future, our lives, our communities and one another, or we are doomed. Together, anything is possible, and everything is achievable.

The solutions will come from the people, and not from on high. Throughout history, the best and most hopeful changes have always come in this way. First, we must be real, and face the dangers and opportunities before us with honesty and courage. Then, we must embrace our power, and act.

As Emerson said, "Words are actions; actions are words." We can begin by reading, listening, discussing and speaking up. When we begin to come together to openly and honestly discuss our shared predicament – and whatever delusions we may harbour, we are, ultimately, all in the same boat – we will find a renewed vividness of life and awareness, and a renewed empowerment that comes from joining together in common cause and kinship with others: we will find our hearts, our spirit, our common sense, our greater dignity and confidence and our power; and from that, more tangible actions will begin to emerge. Above all, unite, and embrace your power. The time is now.

(For further reading, see: Ronald Wright, *A Brief History of Progress*; Jared Diamond, *Collapse*; or, *When Technology Fails*, by Mathew Stein.)

Responses and responsiveness:

From shell-shock, paralysis, denial and despair, to empowerment and action

How do we deal with such enormous problems and challenges? We deal with them by first being real, assessing things for what they are, then taking practical steps as individuals, communities, nations and global alliances to make positive outcomes more likely and more widespread, and the worst outcomes less likely and more minimal. The deer in the headlights response is the worst thing we can do. Shake it off. Let's get moving. Here are some practical suggestions for action. Remember, once we begin to act, and also to connect with one another in common cause, the fear begins to dissipate, and a new and greater power and spirit returns. Connect and act now. You are not alone.

Economic depression:

Economic depression is the least frightening of the three great looming dangers in terms of the threats to human beings on earth. But of course, to respond with complacency would be insane. The danger is real, and it is serious. For most, an economic depression would be a tremendous disaster, especially for people who are unprepared. Most people will suffer terribly without a land base.

First and best precaution: gain access to rural land or urban garden space, either as an individual, a family, a co-op or a community. This may be a last resort, fall-back option for most people, but it is the strongest material security possible, after human solidarity and cooperation. Land is not enough in itself, but it is the primary and first ingredient after human community, solidarity and cooperation for a decent life in difficult times.

If the depression is severe, or there is a full economic collapse, those with land should expect refugees, and start preparing now to take them in. Refusal to share in a time of desperate crisis or disaster will lead at least the violent few to desperate measures. Sharing is sanity. Miserliness is selfish and also self-endangering. These are the basic facts. We can deal with them as we like. As usual, those who choose to deal with reality over fantasy will tend to fare better.

To stand on one's own "property" with a shotgun, or even more firepower, and refuse to help what may well be large numbers of mainly non-violent refugees, would be cruel, inhuman, insane, and a recipe for disaster. Sharing and cooperation are our greatest human strengths, in both good times and bad. If we want to weaken and endanger ourselves, then we should be miserly and look out for ourselves alone. If we want to be as strong and resilient, adaptable and empowered as possible – to say nothing of virtue, compassion or honour – we should find the courage and the heart to share and cooperate with others. Solidarity and adaptability are what got human beings through the last ice age. They are what will get us through the troubles that lay ahead now.

Becoming survivalists, hunkered in our bunkers with caches of weapons and large doses of paranoia and xenophobia would be a recipe for even greater disaster, and is furthermore a royal road to madness. *It is not isolation and weapons that will defend and protect us, but preparation and mutual aid.* We need gardens, not guns; and community, not paranoid isolationism. If you want to survive, and even thrive, open your heart, and share. Help one another, and the road will be easier. Many hands make a light load. What is difficult or impossible for one, is possible, and possibly even easy, with the power of community. Fear is the greatest enemy – not people. The brave will unite in mutual aid. They will be the strongest, in good times and bad.

Remember, you can be tactically smart, and strategically stupid. Stealing a truck and driving it through a K-Mart to grab guns, then robbing your neighbours for supplies may be tactically intelligent, although morally bankrupt: but strategically, it is suicide. He who lives by the sword dies by the sword. It is a round world: sooner or later all our actions come back to us, for better or worse. Smarter it is to be compassionate, kind, and to help one another. In reality, especially in the long term, there are only win-win, or lose-lose scenarios. Compassion and mutual aid are basic intelligence. They represent enlightened self-interest, as well as virtue and nobility.

Remember also: we learn as we go, and adapt on the fly. It is best and wisest to be prepared – the Boy Scouts got that right – but it is impossible to foresee everything.

To make a rather mundane analogy, I just cooked a chicken soup from scratch, for the first time; and it turned out, once it had cooled and steeped overnight for flavour, to be not a soup, or even a stew, but a casserole. Trivial example, I know, but it still serves up a lesson. Too much of one ingredient was added – too many noodles. The result was a thick bland casserole rather than a tasty soup. But I realized that all that was needed was more seasoning to balance out the excess pasta. Once the adaptation was made, the result was wonderful and delicious! So things didn't go as expected – adaptation is 90% of life. Prepare well, and prepare to adapt. There are more serious concerns at stake than chicken soup. Preparation, adaptation, cooperation and goodwill will see us through.

Economic depression or collapse is likely to hit on a global scale, but clearly some regions will fare better and others worse. Some cities, communities and regions are in more dependent positions, and some have found a greater degree of economic independence and resiliency. Some have chosen their allies unwisely; others with more foresight. Nonetheless, despite widely varying degrees of severity, the coming depression or collapse will be global, even if it may not be universal. The BRIC nations – Brazil, Russia, India, China, Mexico, Argentina and others – may come through it, with experiences varying country by country, more unscathed than the formerly rich and dominant European and North American nations, and this seems in fact to be likely.

(The BRIC is rising; the giants are falling. Five centuries of colonialism, neo-colonialism and imperialism seem to have sown their karmic seeds, which are now being reaped – with sad results and a harvest of pain for the people of the fading imperial powers, who generally were quite oblivious to the blood that was on their hands, and the actions that were carried out in their names by their so-called "leaders." Obedience has its consequences. "I was only doing my job, carrying out orders," doesn't cut it with the moral arc of the universe and cosmic justice, unfortunately. There will be major re-adjustments. A global shift is under way. Ozymandias is falling. Help one another, and the transition will be easier and less painful as a new balance is struck.)

Generating economic resources through social entrepreneurship, through value-centred business, to help as many people as possible is my principle response to this looming economic crisis personally; along with warning people and giving them ideas on how to prepare for such an event. I would urge all business-minded people, investors and entrepreneurs to give serious thought to what can be done through economic means to help others. And it is not only kind to direct our energies in such a way: as we have said, it is also intelligent.

I would advise others who want to help, to raise as much money as possible, buy as much land as possible, along with tools and low-cost ecological building materials (such as straw bales and concrete for the proven and low-cost, comfortable, strong and ecological building method of straw bale construction), and provide land and resources for as many people and families as possible. Pooling resources if necessary with friends, family and community members, even very small sums of money can create islands of hope, inspiration and empowerment.

Smarter still, if you have the means, or can find the means, provide land and building materials to create ultra low-cost housing for many, in small ecological villages or tiny hamlets of a few families. And the cost is relatively small – far less than most would imagine, if we are willing to think outside the box, and look to innovative, low-cost, ecological construction methods; and even more so if we pare back a bit of the excessive economic individualism which traps us like rodents on a treadmill, and learn how to cooperate and share. Sharing resources and mutual aid is far more efficient than our current norm of economic individualism, where everybody needs two of their own of everything and has to do everything for themselves.

SHARE! This is not kindergarten: this should not have to be taught again, nor spelled out. It is basic decency, basic morality, and it is also basic sanity or common sense. You will also reap only what you sow. Sow generosity, cooperation, mutual aid and love, and you will be protecting your ass in the most intelligent and effective way possible. Greed is death. Love is life. Share.

We are our brother's keeper. Anyone who says otherwise is, by now, arguably criminally negligent, as well as morally bankrupt, and deeply confused. Share. Again, it is a round world. What you put out, sooner or later comes back to you – whether that be callousness, brutality, aggression or simple coldness; or whether it be warmth, generosity, respect, appreciation and love.

Starting small ecological farming co-ops and villages sounds like a monumental task, even if it is tiny and even if it is just one, but the basics are simple: land, building materials, seeds, garden tools, and human cooperation. Three acres and a small straw bale / stucco cottage per family: one acre to live on and grow a garden to feed your family, and two acres for a market garden, so families can grow flowers, herbs or vegetables for market, so they have some small economic base, in addition to basic self-reliance. One to 10 or 20 families per farm. One hundred straw bales and some concrete per cottage, plus minimal wood for roofing. (Cob building and earth bag construction are even less expensive, and necessitate no lumber or straw bales.) It is not complicated, and it is certainly not rocket science. It is entirely do-able, for those who have the courage, the imagination and the heart.

Even today, prior to economic depression, millions of families in North America are poor enough, desperate enough, and hungry enough, that three acres and a little straw-bale/stucco cottage, with garden space, seeds and garden tools, would seem like a dream come true, or at least an answer to their desperation, and a step up. In the near future, there will be many tens of millions who will jump at such an opportunity. Build now. It is easier to build when the weather is mild, than in the middle of a storm. And this is not even mentioning the global need, which is vastly greater. Build now. Help one another.

To return to the subject of raising funds for such projects, again I am compelled to turn to business and social entrepreneurship. This is the overwhelming motivation and primary goal in pursuing business for me: raise money to help people through the coming storms. Business is the only way I see to raise large amounts of money, in a short time, in order to help as many people as possible. Governments and corporations are a write-off at the moment, with only a few exceptions - they are made up of the blind and the corrupt. Non-profits do wonderful work, but they are continuously limited by a lack of funds, and have to chronically go begging in order to get just a small fraction of the work done which is so urgently needed. Independent business is the only major vehicle I see now for helping the maximum number of people in the shortest possible time. The race is on. A depression would make the task of raising funds to help people by means of business, much more difficult, and possibly impossible. It's now or never. Social entrepreneurs, let's get it going.

In terms of assets, resources and allies that can be counted upon in times of trouble, governments, large corporations, jobs, pay cheques, paper money, banks and bank accounts, safety deposit boxes, rented or leased housing, real estate or homes you don't own outright, gold and silver certificates (as opposed to the actual metal), stocks and bonds, pensions, retirement plans and mutual funds, are all among the least reliable and least secure. Land, tools, seeds, knowledge and skills, wells, cisterns and water systems, green power systems such as wind, solar, geothermal and micro-hydro, and above all, human cooperation and community, are the strongest and most reliable assets, resources and safety nets we can look to or provide for our families and others. In between the most secure and the least secure are community co-ops, credit unions, gold, silver, and certain wisely chosen investments. These things would be wise to bear in mind, and a shift in assets and allies in advance of possible further troubles would be wisest. A lackadaisical attitude of complacency is most dangerous now.

What is likely, if a severe economic crisis or collapse does come – which it looks at present is likely unavoidable – the Western corporate and financial elite and their allies will use the crisis, as they use all crises, whether they be real, fabricated, or deliberately manufactured, to further consolidate and increase their power – politically, economically, and in terms of their already dominant rule over the global financial system.

A new global electronic currency may be imposed – at least upon all nations that accept the regime – and all paper money, gold and silver would be outlawed and confiscated. People would be forced to use their smart cards to buy or sell anything, or to get on a bus, plane, train, cab or boat, to pay their rent, mortgage or utility bill, or to get health care or any kind of government services.

What this would mean would be a further heightened control by the already ruling corporate and financial barons. Everything would be tracked – every purchase and every movement of the people. Worse, dissidents and activists may find that their electronic credits are suspended or cut off, leaving them literally out in the cold to starve.

Accepting such a global cashless society would thus be very unwise, to say the least. The more reliable assets and resources, as outlined above, are far safer – but if repressive measures are taken, these may be very difficult to utilize, unless people are going to try to live entirely without any form of money or currency, or they relocate outside the lock-down zones. (Already, alternative community currencies along with cash transactions in the informal economy are being suppressed. The trend is likely to continue, and to accelerate dramatically.) These are things to consider in advance, if we do not want to be blind-sided.

Beyond the responses laid out above, of course there are many other things that can be done to help our families, communities and others. Activism at all levels is needed. I have focused on two major areas here, since I feel they have the greatest potential to help the most people: community self-reliance; and social entrepreneurship to fund and create sustainable communities.

Choose your path well. The game of musical chairs is coming to a close. The party is over.

Fascism:

1984, Brave New World, We, Brazil, Orwell, Huxley, Zamyantin and many others have tried to warn us. Thomas Jefferson warned us more than 200 years ago, but we did not listen. Now it is here. A dark hour has arrived. And yet, the majority of the people remain locked in a numbed state of paralysis and denial. We had best awaken now. The sop to Cerberus is lost, and the hounds are at the door.

Politics cannot be separated from economics. This should be political-economy 101, but unfortunately, for many this is not yet understood. Politics and economics should be kept at some degree of separation of powers, just as we wisely separated the powers of church and state; but to presume that economics and politics are already, automatically separate realms, is to court disaster. This has been our common assumption since the democratic revolutions of the Enlightenment era in America and France, and this unconscious and unexamined assumption has been our folly. Jefferson saw through it – most of the rest of us did not. For this reason, economics has now taken over the democratic process of the political realm. This is how we ended up in the perilous situation which we now face. Now, we are forced to confront reality. Theory will no longer hold. Reality always holds all the trump cards. And reality is barking at our door, and growling hungrily.

This is not a Marxist analysis, by the way, nor a leftist analysis – it is simply a matter of facing the facts which stare us directly in the face. It is a matter of using our common sense, and dealing with the obvious and undeniable realities that stand before us now. Our democracy has been hijacked, and is in the final stages of a process of complete disembowelment and evisceration. It is not new in history, but it cannot be ignored – at least not without great peril.

After World War II, the people of the Western world lived in a mixture of jubilant triumphalism, grief, mourning, trauma and shell-shock. It was not just the horrors of war that left us in such a state of trauma and shock, but even more so, the horrors of fascism, and the brutalities that were witnessed and endured by human beings on this Earth by mad, tyrannical powers gone out of control. As the trauma slowly began to heal, over decades and generations, the majority of people slipped quietly into a complacent state of denial. Legions of veterans tried yearly to warn us, lest we forget, but we forgot – we insisted on telling ourselves that it could not happen again. Above all, we insisted on telling ourselves that it could not happen here. But our very complacency and lack of vigilance allowed just such patterns to begin to arise once more. Now, it is happening again. Fascism is at our doorstep.

Being awake to the dangers now would be extremely wise. They may yet be averted, and we would be smart to do everything in our power to prevent such appalling and horrific conditions from emerging again. In any event, to face the future with open eyes is most intelligent. The wilfully blind tend always to suffer the most, and their chosen blindness further endangers us all. It is now time for a large dose of reality. We will have it one way or another, quite soon – it may as well be sooner than later, for sooner is far safer, and far more empowering. Again, continuing denial is the greatest danger we face.

We already live under corporate rule. Everyone who is paying attention knows it. Most people are aware of the fact, even if they would prefer to deny it, or simply to not think about it. We are now moving from corporate rule to corporate fascism. Some would say, what's the difference? The difference is great. While corporate rule may be abhorrent – unjust, war-like, unecological and anti-democratic – corporate fascism is nothing short of a nightmare.

The few hundred international business elites and family dynasties who control the biggest corporations already dominate the global economy, as well as the major political parties, the political process and the media. They are now consciously and deliberately consolidating their power, while they can, knowing full well that they are in the midst of a deep, widespread and growing crisis of legitimacy. Before the rug is pulled out from under them and they lose all power, they want to consolidate their power, so that they hopefully never lose it. This means making sure that they or their cronies are securely entrenched in power, and all forms of dissent and all vestiges of democracy, along with the power of the people, are dutifully strangled or drowned.

What is fascism? Fascism does not necessarily mean goose-stepping soldiers in the street, or racism or skin heads. Contemporary fascism is multi-cultural, and has made itself very well camouflaged under a guise of respectability – as mob bosses have learned to do – with a thick layer of Orwellian populist, pseudo-democratic window dressings. Fascism today is run, not out of the offices of the heads of state, but the closed door clubs of the business elite who control them. Washington, London, Paris and Berlin could fall off the map entirely, and the Western fascist regime would continue along, virtually unaffected. The centres of power are the financial districts and remote, exclusive resorts, not the political capitals of yesteryear.

Fascism has many flavours and hides behind many different masks, but essentially, it is this. Fascism is the merger of business and the state, as Mussolini himself defined it. The business elite and the powers of the state are united and fused together, and democracy is kicked to the curb, since it is a nuisance and a barrier to straight, unfettered elite rule. Democracy means rule by the people. Elite rule is the defining characteristic of fascism, above every other trait. The two are utterly incompatible and antithetical. When one enters, the other must leave or be crushed. Fascism is entering our society now, and this is the case for Europe, North America, and many other parts of the world that are already under a pseudo-democratic corporate dominance, and are moving rapidly toward the full destruction of democracy, regardless of the rhetoric and the spin.

Remember also, when democracy is destroyed, human rights and freedom go with it. There is no such thing as a kind, gentle, or just fascism. It is the rule of the elite, by the elite, for the elite – everyone else be damned.

Look at Italy: Italy already had a right-wing, neoconservative/neoliberal pro-corporate, pro-banker government, but that was considered to be not enough by the international business and financial elite. Pressure came from the EU, ECB, IMF and the banking elite to make more radical changes, in line with the interests of the financial elite. Now Italy is ruled directly by the bankers, and there is not even a pretence of anything other. There are killer attack drones used within the United States itself now – not only will the empire be defended with high tech lethal force, but so too will the heartland of the empire. Not surprising, but very chilling, and still, few people dare call this fascism. The NDAA was passed and approved by Obama, making it legal for anyone in the U.S. or anywhere else to be indefinitely detained and imprisoned for life, be they American citizens or anyone else. And yet none dare call it fascism. The Military Commissions Act was passed a few years ago, making torture and summary execution legal. And yet none dared call it fascism. The Patriot Act was passed shortly before that, rendering the Constitution and Bill of Rights null and void, and yet it seems, a majority of people carried on as if nothing had happened, no big changes had occurred, and everything was the ordinary boring banality of a hollowed out democracy, but still a democracy.

We do not live in a democracy. Fascism is here. How much does it take to get us to accept the obvious which is now staring us in the face? And the screw tightens daily, and the people yawn. Danger looms, and it seems that most are determined to sleepwalk to the gulag or the gallows.

(If there is any doubt as to the swiftly emerging dark reality of fascism, see Geralde Celente, the leading trend analyst in the world. Or see Naomi Wolf, or countless others who are sounding the very necessary alarm.)

Fascism is truly hideous and terrifying. It is not like other crises, which are frightening enough in themselves. With ecological or economic crises, the great majority of people naturally help one another, and although the suffering is great, the mutual aid pulls us through. With fascism, mutual aid is shattered, as the people are deliberately divided and isolated in mutual mistrust and fear, so that the elite can rule unimpeded by the people, who, if they got together, would quickly overthrow the tyranny which oppresses and exploits them. With mutual aid and human cooperation being thwarted and blocked, actively discouraged and undermined, the people drift in terrified numbness and isolation, as the madness and darkness of evil reigns. Sooner or later, the people come out of their state of shock, and throw off their oppressors, but it usually takes a few years, historically, before this happens. In the meantime, life under fascism is a bleak and grim wasteland – dispiriting, demoralizing, brutal and crushing to any who have their hearts and minds still alive.

The only responses to fascism, in the short-term, are three: prevent its full emergence and defeat it in advance – which I have tried to do, by warning people, and urging them to stand up for their rights, their freedom and their democracy, and which we should all seek to do with every ounce of our power; escape it – which means, get out of the way of this short-lived but hideous, all-crushing giant, and possibly fight it from a safe distance and a place of strength (remember, David needed some distance from Goliath to sling his small stone and bring the giant down); or wait it out – which means, realistically, waiting until the people are ready to throw it off, and possibly building a resistance movement to prepare for that time, while waiting under the crushing weight and all-encompassing brutality.

We are running out of time for option one. The beast is very nearly upon us. Options one and two are very fast closing their window of opportunity. Move now, in whatever way you feel is best. Time is running out. Let us do everything in our power to prevent this horror, and think well of places of strength from which to fight it, if it is not prevented in time.

The horror of a fully emerged fascism can yet be averted. It is not too late, but we must act now. We should also prepare in case it does succeed in taking full power, and think hard on what our plan of response might be. If it does arise in its hideous fullness, it will not last. All empires fall. This present global corporate order will fall as well. A renaissance is being born, and no reactionary power will stop it. However, to prevent the worst, and to prevent even a short-term descent into the horrors of totalitarianism, we must act now. Boldness, basic human decency and common sense, along with the power of unity within diversity, are our greatest strengths, and we need to bring them forth now.

Ecological disaster and collapse:

I will not elaborate in detail here what we must do to avert further ecological disaster or collapse. It has been covered well by others, in many other works. Excellent information is available from the Sierra Club, Greenpeace,

Friends of the Earth, New Society Publishers, the David Suzuki Foundation, the World Watch Institute and other organizations. David Suzuki and Jeremy Rifkin, among others, are particularly lucid and knowledgeable on the subject.

To outline in brief what must be done in terms of preventing further ecological disaster or collapse, and to move towards and create a truly sustainable world, we can say this. We have to make major shifts in food, land and resource distribution, health care and education. This is necessary not only to eliminate poverty for reasons of justice and compassion: eliminating poverty and providing universal education is the primary necessity and proven means for population stabilization. All of the international development organizations know this. It has been proven abundantly. Share the wealth and eliminate poverty, or watch the world burn. There is no third option. Neo-Malthusianism is hideously callous and inhuman, as well as delusional and insane.

Along with more fairly distributing the wealth and resources of the earth, we must also make major shifts in our agriculture and food systems, energy and transportation systems, manufacturing and production, materials use, resource use and allocation, housing and construction – and in our communities, lives and nations, in all of these areas.

We must shift our emphasis from material consumption and status based upon the accumulation and hoarding of wealth, to quality of life, and social esteem and pride based upon helping one another and living a meaningful life. "Simplify, share and enjoy," must replace "gather, hoard and flaunt."

We need to diminish our over-emphasis on economic individualism, and shift the balance more toward sharing. Car co-ops and mass transit are far more efficient and ecological, for example, than having every home or family have one or two vehicles of their own.

Homes and buildings must be made far more energy efficient. Energy efficiency and conservation are primary. All buildings should be super energy efficient and passive solar, with supplemental geothermal heating and cooling, whether by design or by retrofit, wherever possible, as well as energy self-reliant, producing actual surpluses of electricity to feed into the power grid for use by factories, office buildings and schools. We also need to shift our energy use and transportation patterns from fossil fuels and nuclear power, to clean, renewable green energy, such as wind, solar, geothermal, co-generation, wave, tidal and micro-hydro, using clean-burning hydrogen fuel and hydrogen fuel cells as energy storage and transport systems.

We need to shift from toxic and non-renewable materials, such as plastics and synthetics, in all our manufacturing, production and consumption, to non-toxic, renewable materials, such as sustainable yield wood and bamboo, stone, stucco, clay, straw, adobe, hemp composites, recycled steel, organic cotton, leather, hemp and wool. And we need a wholesale conversion from our present, utterly unsustainable and highly toxic petrochemical industrial agriculture to organic food and farming.

We also need a major reduction in meat and dairy consumption, as well as in per capita energy use. Protection of wildlands and water systems, as well as reforestation and the regeneration of ecosystems, are also vitally necessary.

Additionally, while some aspects of globalization, such as the global sharing of information, culture and ideas, are excellent and beneficial to human beings and life on earth, other aspects decidedly are not. Having the great majority of our goods manufactured in China and shipped all around the world, is neither socially nor ecologically wise, nor even feasible in the long term. Dependence on highly centralized power systems, such as oil wells, coal mines and fossil fuel or nuclear power plants, is both dangerous socially, in terms of overly centralizing power in society, and also ecologically. Allowing a handful of giant corporations to control the global economy is both socially disastrous as well as ecologically unsound. Distributed or decentralized, community and home-based green energy is the shift we need. Similarly, a re-localization and decentralization of manufacturing and production, as well as economics generally, is both more ecological and also more democratic than the current system of global supply lines and globalized control over production and economics. Rebuild community and decentralize production, energy and economic power, or a dark, dystopian, Dickensian age of barrens dotted by walled islands of wealth, will be our future. We can see the trend already. It has to be denied wilfully to be ignored.

But this is only the briefest sketch. More will be said on these topics later.

In terms, not of preventing ecological disaster or collapse, but of preparation in case it should happen, the notes listed for preparation for a possible economic collapse apply and overlap here to a large degree. Community self-reliance is a primary strategy, for any who want to be truly well prepared in case of such an event, or cascade of events. If we allow the unfolding ecological crisis to reach the cataclysmic levels it certainly will reach if we do not act swiftly, the global economy will collapse, infrastructure will collapse, nations will fall, and cities will crumble to ruin. Smaller communities, closely tied to the land and with an agricultural base, will tend to survive. Rugged individualists in most cases will not.

Communities can become, must become, and quite probably will be forced to become much more self-reliant in the near future. There is much that has been written on the subject, and much thought and experimentation and modelling that has been done. Community self-reliance, combined with federations and alliances among communities for trade, the sharing of information and ideas, mutual aid, protection and disaster relief, will become increasingly important, and quite possibly essential. Much can be done by individuals and families, and also at the level of states and nations, but it will most likely be at the level of the community that preparedness and effective ability to respond will be most possible and also most critical – *if* communities use forethought, and think ahead, that is.

Again, this is just a brief outline of responses that can be taken. Much more is yet to come. The central aim of this article was not so much to lay out plans for responding to the greatest threats facing humanity, but to clarify those threats, as a starting point. First, honestly assess the situation or the risk; then a clear plan of action can be formed – not before.

(For further details on related subjects see Mathew Stein's book, *When Technology Fails*. It is an excellent resource manual on disaster preparedness. It should be in every home, office, school and library. Every community leader and every citizen should be familiar with it, and have it on hand.)

Plans of action are detailed in further articles and essays in the book. This is just an overview and a summary of some of the greatest challenges ahead. We need broad strokes, a big picture view, before we can flesh out the details – otherwise, we are forever unable to see the forest for the trees; and that is a tragic and epidemic condition that we should not wish to continue with any longer. Big picture first, then zoom in to look at the finer details, otherwise we live as Mister Magoo.

Like Mister Magoo, with our habitual and learned short-sightedness, it is a wonder that we haven't fallen even more into mishaps and self-wounding than we have. It is time to correct our myopia now, before we terminate our existence, and that of most species on the planet along with us.

A summary of thoughts on sensible responsiveness:

Ecological crisis leading to civilizational collapse, almost looks like a picnic compared to fascism. Yes, it will be messy, to say the least, and yes, there will be suffering – major suffering – but the people will help one another, more or less, and generally more than less. We will get through it if it happens, and we will get through it better if we embrace *three basic principles* – and all three principles pertain and relate, and are relevant and highly important, with regard to any social, political or economic danger or crisis, by the way, and not only to ecological crisis.

1. **Deal with reality** – don't play games of fantasy or denial. Deal with what is, what is unfolding, and what dangers are looming, however probable or improbable, imminent or distant they may appear to be.

2. **Be prepared and be proactive.** Take action now – in terms of both prevention and preparation. Don't wait for disaster to put together your disaster plan. Communities, cities and governments all over the world have begun creating disaster response plans. Families need them too, for communities, cities and governments are often overwhelmed in times of disaster, and it is up to the people to help themselves and one another – witness hurricane Katrina. Be prepared. Now. Not in five years, or next year, but now. Increase your preparedness as well as your knowledge at whatever speed you can, daily, monthly or at least yearly. DON'T BE COMPLACENT. Do everything in your power to avert these looming disasters; and prepare now in case we fail to avert them completely or in time. God grant that we may avert them. It is not too late, but time is perilously thin.

3. **Help one another.** Your karma and also your ass are dependent upon how well you cooperate with others and generously help one another. As a loner, you are in trouble, and in danger. This is only more and more true every day. In times of crisis or disaster, it is doubly true. Help one another, or be prepared to sink or swim alone, and with much worse odds. Love and mutual aid are the keys to happiness and not only to survival. Get it together by getting together with others: help one another – now, and not when it is too late. In a word, don't be greedy, and don't think that looking out for number one is a smart survival strategy, or an intelligent path to a happy life. It is dumb. Be smart. Help one another. We are far more powerful together than we are alone.

Conclusion

1. Do what you can to avert these disasters – there is much that can be done individually, and a tremendous amount collectively. Act now. Everything is possible if the people are bold, and they unite.

Normally this would be priority one, and it still is: avert these disasters. Failing that, we fall back to priority two: prepare for the onslaught, and to avoid or weather the storm, while helping one another all we can, and sowing the seeds for a better world.

I am afraid we may be too late to avert at least the economic and ecological disasters now – we have been too complacent, too passive, and frankly, too docile and cowardly, and have avoided reality for too long. Now, reality is about to bite us on the ass, I am afraid. Prepare yourself. And remember, a hard rain doesn't last all day.

We will overcome all obstacles to peace and mutual prosperity, in freedom and democracy and ecological sanity – but it may take some time. If the people rally now, and strongly enough, then the worst can be avoided. I am still urging that we do all we can to avoid the worst. We should, however, also be prepared for the consequences if the people remain passive, and allow the worst of the looming disasters to fully unfold – which they very well may choose to do. Raise your voice, and do what you can. You are not alone.

We will defeat the darkness that is rising now, even if it does take some time. There will be a new day for humanity, and a brighter day yet to come.

2. Prepare now for the possible arising of these three social and ecological disasters, which are undeniable, presently gathering storms; storms which we the people, may or may not effectively avert, and which may hit with full force very soon: economic depression or collapse; fascism; and civilizational collapse due to ecological cataclysm. We must boldly work for change, and also, prepare in case we have a temporary or partial failure.

It seems to me to come down to prevention, preparation, amelioration, and moving through. Work for prevention above all; but also spend some serious time and effort on preparation, in case the worst does unfold. If it does, we will need and want to ameliorate the damage and the suffering, and to shorten the time of the hardship; and we will need a clear vision and strategy for moving through the difficult times, and building a new and better world. All four are necessary and vital now.

Some may call it karma, some will call it fate, others will call it divine agency – I would prefer to simply say that the troubles that are brewing are a matter of cause and effect. We have set certain patterns into motion, creating the causes for certain possible, or in some cases, probable events. Generally speaking, we did not set such harmful patterns into motion out of evil, but due to ignorance. Other patterns have been allowed to emerge, grow and gather force, and it is our inaction which is allowing them now to threaten humanity and the earth with great peril. And there are still other patterns in motion which are simply beyond our control. Overall, however, the situation remains the same: what we do or do not do matters. We are not mere spectators of life. We are actively engaged in the shaping of our individual and collective futures, every moment and every day. This time is no different in that regard. The only difference is, the stakes are higher. The dangers are real, and so too are the opportunities for major positive change. What ensues is largely up to us.

Warn people, and take action now. If we do not avert these disasters, then we will be forced to deal with them when they arise in full form. Better always to be prepared.

Don't be fatalistic – but do be prepared, in case the worst does arise. Hope for the best, prepare for the worst. Preparation is wise. Prudence is sanity. Compassionate action is responsibility, and also enlightened self-interest.

Denial is madness and extreme peril, as well as cowardly irresponsibility to one's fellow human beings. Act now.

If we are strong and brave and reasonably sane, we will avoid all three of these great disasters – or at least the last and worst two, which are on the near horizon as we speak. If we are not, then we will have no choice but to suffer through them, and deal with them as they come. Hopefully the former is the case, but the future is uncertain, and is in our hands.

Ultimately, humanity will experience a renaissance, which is also emerging now. Whether we experience a short period of great darkness between now and then, remains to be seen, and is yet to be decided. To paraphrase that marvellously lucid statesman, George H. W. Bush, we are the deciders.

It is up to us. We are the makers of our future. And the critical moment is now. Be brave. A new day is dawning. Real change, positive change for the world we live in, and for human beings and all living beings, will come, and is unfolding now. Whether we have to live through further darkness or nightmarish scenarios before it is attained, or whether our transition to a better world is a transition that is more one of peace, is up to us, and what we do now – right now.

Make a move. The time is now. Act.

Remember, it is not all or nothing – it is not black and white. Everything we do matters. Every life and every moment matters – matters profoundly. All life matters, or nothing matters. And the latter view is a paralyzing and bleak nihilistic self-delusion. Life matters, whatever the outcome.

Remember too, that all things are impermanent. This too shall pass. Stay calm, stay confident, stay warm, and do all you can. And try to be at peace with that.

When it all gets too dark, too heavy or too overwhelming, as it sometimes may, take a break. Put on Bach or James Taylor, take a walk in the woods or spend some time by the water. Remember to appreciate the beauty and goodness in life. It is there, and it nourishes us, if we will but slow down enough to take notice and appreciate it. Go dancing, do yoga or meditation, or just sit with a cup of coffee or tea and enjoy the sunshine or the rain. Cook a hearty, wholesome meal – slowly, and enjoy both the process as well as the result. Better yet: share the process and the feast, however modest or elaborate. Burn-out helps no one, and being strung out, frazzled, tense, depressed or obsessed isn't helpful either.

Remember that the samurai of Japan were trained in flower arranging, calligraphy, poetry and philosophy – and with good reason. In order to give birth to a renaissance, we must become renaissance men and women – which means, among other things, that we must cultivate a more balanced life than is the norm in our current society.

A balanced life helps not only ourselves, but also others, and makes us more effective in all we do, as well as more clear-minded and powerful. Take a break when you need to, then return to the task at hand. We're in it for the long haul. Nourish your body, mind and spirit. It is necessary and it is wise. Savour every victory, and every act of kindness and courage, no matter how small, and never surrender. Keep on dancing into the light. A new world is being born, and we are her midwives. Let the work of creating a better world be joyful. It need not be dour. It can be an act of joy.

Grieve for the past. Make space for the future, and especially the present. We are all wounded. Grieving clears away the clouds of pain and fear, helps us to see more clearly, opens the heart, and opens us up to create again and start afresh.

Remember that everyone suffers, and everyone wishes to be happy: we are more alike than we are different. We are one family. The only true enemy is ignorance.

This is not a declaration of war. It is a declaration of healing. We are creating a better world for all – through an open and inclusive democratic process that uplifts and empowers, ennobles and dignifies all; a process of rebirth and renewal that honours the innate dignity of all living beings and all individuals. That does not mean that firmness and boldness are not necessary: they are. But we must keep the perspective and the goal in mind. This is about the healing of our world.

Remember above all, the future is in our hands. The world is what we make of it.

It is time for us to begin the world anew.

JTR
June 5, 2012

THE IRRELEVANCE OF THE STATE

I'M NOT SURE ABOUT acting as if the state is irrelevant or doesn't matter, as some have suggested – the state *does* matter. Love it or hate it, we cannot avoid it. I like Chomsky's view, and Thoreau's. Both are anarchists, or left libertarians, and both are very lucid in their practicality as far as both short-term and long-term objectives.

Thoreau spells it out in his essay, "On Civil Disobedience." "I heartily agree with that motto, that government is best which governs the least; and I should like to see it acted up to more readily and more fully; and I would extend it to say this: that government is best which governs not at all – and when are prepared for it, that is precisely the kind of government they shall have." He then clarifies that he is no head-in-the-clouds idealist, but an idealist with his feet firmly on the ground. "But I do not count myself among the no-government men... I do not wish for, at once no government, but at once a better government. Let every man state what kind of government would command his respect, and that shall be one step towards attaining it." I agree on both counts completely.

Chomsky echoes the same sentiments of long term and short term vision and goals, almost precisely, as does Bertrand Russell. Along with Thoreau, these are three of the most lucid political thinkers I have ever encountered.

Chomsky is explicit that even if we are critical of the state and its power, we would be unwise to try to dispense with it just yet: the business elite rule society, and the state is the one institutional power that is strong enough and that the people could potentially use to oppose this domination and correct it. For that reason, he feels we should have a clear-eyed and intelligent, limited support of the state, when and where it can be used to express the power of the people, through democracy, to oppose rule by economic or other elites and serve the many rather than the few.

Generally speaking, I think these three great thinkers are right. We should be seeking to renew and strengthen democracy, not dismiss the state as irrelevant. National democracies are our first and best hope in defending against an all-out assault by generally ruthlessly exploitative and truly oppressive business elites, and should not be abandoned, but instead transformed and revitalized, and made genuinely democratic.

Chomsky makes clear that in his view, we should aim for reforms, or short-term goals, and use the small victories, build upon them, to strive for greater triumphs. "We should expand the floor of the cage," he said, "with the view of breaking out of it, once we've created the basis for going beyond." To pretend we are not in a cage, to pretend that we are not subjugated by a confluence of state and corporate power, which have by now been merged, is not liberating, but simply delusional. As a general rule, I think it is safe to say that we should start by dealing with reality, not avoiding it. State power is real: it cannot be avoided nor dismissed, and to ignore it is simply perilous and also irresponsible. The state will continue to negatively affect the world until we transform it. It cannot be ignored.

Whether we believe that the state can be brought under democratic control to serve the interests of the people or not, the state cannot be ignored, for it is the second most influential centre of power after the reigning economic elites.

The state must be resisted when it is a usurped tool of a self-serving, anti-democratic ruling elite, as with Stalinist Russia, Nazi Germany or corporatist present day; or else captured by a truly populist democratic movement and made to serve the interests of the people – one or the other, or both: but it cannot be ignored nor dismissed.

The only thing that I can see that would make sense from that line of thought – the thought that the state can somehow be dismissed as irrelevant – is not dismissing or ignoring the state at all, but focusing primarily elsewhere, considering that the state has been captured by the ruling corporate elite, and that inroads to regaining even a semblance of popular democratic control would be difficult.

Focusing on grassroots efforts makes a great deal of sense to me. Building community, solidarity and better alternatives, working models, on the ground at the level of the grassroots to aid, empower, unite and inspire the people, is an important, if not the most important task at hand. Addressing the state and the corporate hegemony both, must, I think, go along with that.

JTR
February 2012

BLIND-SPOTS OF THE LEFT

L ET ME START BY pissing everybody off, right from the beginning, by saying unequivocally that neither the left nor the right has all the answers, and in fact, both are highly caught up in group think and unquestionable assumptions, blindly following their respective leaders as if they were messiahs. Having offended everyone equally, maybe we can get down to business, so to speak, and deal with some very important issues: issues of collective blind-spots in our thinking and awareness – and by our, I mean human beings, and not any one particular group.

I will address the blind-spots of the left in particular here, however, for the simple reason that my views would most commonly be associated with the left, or with progressives, or whatever currently fashionable term we might like to use, and so the larger part of the audience for my writings, although far from the entirety of it I would hope, is likely to be among the left. And for all its glories and triumphs, the left does indeed have its downfalls, short-comings and obstacles – and not all of them are externally caused! Ahem...

The natural human impulse toward living as social animals is our greatest strength and also our greatest weakness. When it manifests as our greatest strength, it is a natural inclination or impulse towards empathy, compassion, cooperation and mutual aid– which is what allowed us to survive without claws, fangs, body armour, or great speed or strength through the millennia, and also to thrive and become the pre-eminent species on the planet.

Think of a barn raising, the creation of the internet or iPad, the ending of apartheid, the gaining of universal suffrage or the moon landing: virtually everything significant that has been accomplished by human beings has been accomplished through a joint effort of shared vision, cooperation and common cause; and when a cooperative effort was not absolutely necessary, as it is for anything of large scale or complexity, then it is certainly an enormous benefit to help one another, even if we could potentially do it alone. Even great scientific or artistic accomplishments, which would seem on the surface to be the work of single individuals, have virtually always relied, directly or indirectly, on human solidarity and cooperation. As Newton said himself, "If I have seen further, it is because I have stood on the shoulders of giants." In virtually every endeavour, from science to the arts, to business, politics or the humanities, we owe a tremendous amount to the fact of our human instinct towards cooperation and working together. This is our greatest strength.

However, when our natural instinct to live as social animals manifests as our greatest weakness, as it often does, the social impulse to stick with the herd leads us into a confused and self-disempowering mistrust of ourselves and our own judgement, and causes us to slip into a largely unconscious habit of conformity of thought and action. It is in such a mode of consciousness that human beings become sheep, their common sense and power are squelched, and slavish obedience, group think and mob rule becomes the norm. We become the wooden men, the hollow men, and life becomes fraught with great peril, even while it becomes lifeless, and we are more dead than alive.

We must guard against this latter pattern of following the herd at all costs, and refusing to trust our own judgment and common sense; and draw forth from within us the former, the empowered and confident impulse towards mutual aid, if we wish to see the best in us prevail, and not the worst. This applies to all human beings of course, whatever our political views or inclinations may be.

So why does the left have blind-spots, if indeed, we are willing to admit that it does have some? I would suggest there are a number of reasons, and among them are the following. And again, most if not all of these observations apply to all areas of human society, and people of any and all political inclinations – some more than others. (I have seen many anarchists and libertarians who are more rabid followers of the herd, worshippers of demigods and messiah figures, and more stubborn adherents to blind, unthinking ideology and dogmatism than the most ardent conservative or liberal. The susceptibility to various forms of confusion and ordinary madness is universal; and not the domain of any one group alone.)

Human beings are basically good, despite the cynicism which is often presented as informed opinion. Dignity combined with a clear-eyed honesty is something to strive for, and will help us all.

Some of the reasons for blind-spots in our thinking and awareness as human beings:

1. Group-think

It is not just the right that is vulnerable to group-think, or the often wishy-washy, stick-with-the-pack centre. The left is also vulnerable to group-think. If the herd, or one's own subculture, social group or mini-herd thinks one thing, it tends to be very difficult for us to think another, or even to question the thinking of the herd.

Call it group-think or call it conformity, but it is a common failing of human beings, and having a certain particular ideological disposition does not guarantee immunity. We are hard-wired to be social animals, and we are terrified, at some deep, unconscious existential level, of losing the support of the tribe or clan, upon which we depend to survive; and so, we are terrified of being ostracized, and this terror leads to an unconscious instinct to conform at all costs.

This unconscious conformity applies to both behaviour and to thought, and exists in all social groups, from anarchists to social democrats, liberals, conservatives, libertarians and progressives, to Friedmanite neo-cons or neo-liberals. Of course, habitual conformity of thought, belief and action is more prevalent, to some degree, among people who believe in very authoritarian or elitist structures of power, but it exists among self-professed libertarians and anarchists as well.

In short, blind conformity and group-think is a human weakness, and it is present to some degree just about everywhere. To make matters worse, our society conditions us daily, as well as from birth, to be unthinking conformist drones, mindless busy-bodies and worker bees, who will follow the herd at all costs. It is surprising, considering all this, that we can think at all. But we do, and we muddle through, exercising our natural intelligence and our innate common sense, a little more and more as humanity begins to slowly awaken, as if from a dream. (I am using the term herd here to drive the point home. When we cease to behave as cattle, then I will use a softer word. Presently, we behave as cattle far too often. And yes, that means progressives and people on the left as well as the right, unfortunately.)

While writing this short essay I stopped for a break, to sit in the sun on my front porch and get some fresh air, and three young girls walked by – a young Asian girl and two young black girls of maybe twelve or fourteen years old, singing as they walked; and I thought, what a beautiful friendship, and I prayed that they would always share such wonderful friendship all their lives. Such a natural impulse toward solidarity and kinship is our most precious gift as human beings. We should try at all times to keep it in its best form, and not let it descend into its more confused and harmful patterns of unthinking pack mentality.

2. Follow-the-leader:
the habit of submission to authority

Again, like the impulse to stick with the herd, the impulse to cow tow blindly to authority figures or presumed leaders is a common failing of human beings, and is present in essentially all social groups, including those on the left. The left has its own authorities it bows down to, just as the centre and right do.

The centre will bow down in self-lobotomizing deference to the New York Times, while the right will defer uncritically to Friedman or Hayek (neo-liberals and neo-cons alike bow to these perceived demigods of "free market" fantasies), and the left will tend to bow to its own perceived leaders. When one of our leaders says or writes or thinks something, the unconscious and highly conditioned, socially conditioned response, tends to be, "Ok, that must be true – because so and so said it." We have to break out of this straight-jacket of habitual conformity and deference to authority, and it is not enough simply to shift which authorities we defer to. We must learn once again, to trust ourselves, and to exercise our own judgment, using our natural intelligence and our innate common sense.

This doesn't mean that we should treat all opinions or views as equal of course – obviously they are not. Nor does it mean we should start to shun or reject the views of the most influential of individuals, or stop listening to our best minds or bravest hearts – that would be incredibly foolish and terribly self-defeating. Instead, we should strike a balance in our attitudes between respect for those we perceive as elders, mentors or leaders, and respect for ourselves and our own innate intelligence.

In other words, we must learn to listen with receptivity, openness and respect, and then to use our own minds and hearts to form our own views and determine our own course of action. These things we do need to remind ourselves, for our culture and society tend to condition us in opposite ways: to habitual deference to authority, habitual conformity to the social group or the society, and habitual denial of our own innate intelligence and common sense. We must learn how to balance a legitimate respect for legitimate leadership, with a self-dignity, self-respect, and trust in our own innate intelligence and basic goodness.

3. Financial or material dependency

Financial dependency of many left and progressive media outlets upon, not necessarily corporate funding or corporate advertising dollars, but on government funds, or on funds from foundations, many of which are tied either to the state or to large, powerful corporate interests, seriously undermines independence of thought, expression and action, just as it does with the centre and the right. If we think money can't buy influence, we are sadly mistaken. Most people on the grassroots left as well as the right now understand very well that money can and does buy influence – in the media, the political arena, the academy and elsewhere.

What we tend to deny is that money has any bearing or influence on the media *we watch* – or read, or listen to. The sad fact of the matter is that it does, more often than we think, or would like to imagine. This may not necessarily destroy the independence or quality of left or progressive or any other media entirely, but it certainly can and does limit what gets discussed, what gets downplayed or blacked out, and what opinions, questions or views can and cannot be voiced, printed or aired.

The mass media networks in general are all owned or controlled by either corporate giants or governments. The ones that are not, such as PBS or TVO, tend to be dependent upon large amounts of funding from, and hence are highly influenced and controlled by, the same corporate giants that control most of the media.

Alternative media are supposed to be different, and while they do tend to have more independence, if they are not financially independent, then they are likely limited in the scope and also the presentation of subjects and opin-ions, to at least some degree. This is the unfortunate reality, and it must be acknowledged, so that we can recognize the blind-spots, the self-censorship, or the actual bias or spin, when and where they occur. (The refusal within the "alternative media" to make any serious criticism of the Obama adminis-tration is a glaring example of group think, and simple moral and intellectual cowardice; and one would also expect, at least at times, of funding issues: follow the money – Move On and the Democratic Party are often linked here, and wield real clout.)

Self-censorship is present among left, progressive and alternative media, just as it is across the political spectrum, and is far more common than is imag-ined or admitted. Financial independence is difficult, but should be sought. And when government or foundation money is received by *any* media outlet that claims to be free and open, as with direct corporate "donations," this funding should be made public, and highly visible, as a matter of standard policy and practice. (Just as a "contact" link should appear at the bottom of every web page, so too should a "full-disclosure" link appear visibly at the bottom of the website of every respectable progressive or independent media outlet, linking to a web page that shows full disclosure of all grants, funds, donations or other monies or gifts received from any group, corporation or foundation, or any contribution from an individual that is of considerable size.) For the time being, people on the left, right or centre should be aware that even what appear to be the best sources or media outlets, may have a leash around their necks. That leash may be short or long, but it is still a leash, and the resulting media content is not without filters or bias.

4. Simple corruption –
or far more common, co-option

It is true, believe it or not: progressives and people on the left are not above all human weaknesses. I know, I know – it is shocking, but it is the truth. And sometimes the weaknesses are not small, but very large and very serious: some people do sell their convictions and their values down the river, if the price is right, or the threat is sufficient. Other times, individuals become co-opted, and although their values may remain sincerely intact, their views have become skewed, essentially by being suckered into a position that compromises their values; and they are unable or unwilling to see the contradiction.

These things happen. Most people are sincere; some are not. Most people are not on anybody's payroll, other than in the obvious and honest ways, that is, and not in some hidden or back-door manner – but some are. We can't let such things make us paranoid, nor cause division or suspicion among us, but we need to be aware that such things do occasionally occur, and that plants are present in places other than window sills and flower beds. CONITELPRO is not dead, and nor are corruption or co-option. The majority may be legitimate, and are, but there are certainly a few who are not.

5. Ego

Nobody likes to admit they are wrong. It is a common cognitive error as well as an emotional error that human beings make, and that we must admit to: that when we commit to a certain view, we tend to reinforce that view, to rationalize and justify and entrench it, rather than to question it. It is uncomfortable to even consider that we may be wrong, or may have been mistaken. And when it is a publicly made statement of views, the desire to avoid being wrong intensifies a hundred-fold.

Once we have staked our identity to a publicly stated view for some time, we become increasingly reluctant to admit that we were wrong. The less self-trust and self-confidence we have, ironically, the bigger the ego-attachment. You can tell when someone has a deep well of confidence, for that person has no qualms with admitting that they were mistaken, and changing or amending their views. The converse is also true.

If our ego attachment is large, we will be the most pig-headed ideologue and opinionated bastard in the room, if for no other reason than for the sake of never wanting to have to admit that we were wrong; which means that we never want to change our minds.

Ego exists in all groups, and to some extent, in just about all of us. We must work to overcome it, and to recognize it in ourselves, and gently correct it when we see it. Specifically, with regards to blind-spots, we need to recognize that we all have them, that none of us are omniscient yet, and that it is ok to be wrong, and to admit that we were wrong. As Ralph Waldo Emerson said, "A foolish consistency is the hobgoblin of little minds."

It is alright to change our minds! When new evidence or new information comes up, and it shows a better way, or a more refined view than what we previously had subscribed to, it would be sheer foolishness to reject it, simply because we are emotionally and intellectually ensconced in a view to which we have become fondly, perhaps deeply and perhaps egoically attached. We are learning all the time – or we should be. And more importantly, we are *unlearning* our illusions all the time. When we become fully enlightened and omniscient, then we will have no more illusions; until then, we are always both learning and unlearning, and that is fine, that is normal, that is natural, and that is good!

We should pride ourselves, if anything, on our willingness and openness to considering new information and new ideas, along with a basic good-heartedness. When our minds have turned to stone, then there is something to be embarrassed about. When we are curious and open to new thoughts and new perspectives, that is a good thing!

6. Idolatry of ideology

Clinging to our ideas is another common human weakness. We like our ideas, and quite apart from any ego identification with them, we tend not to want to change them or part with them. This is simple dogmatism, and it is blinding.

We must bear in mind at all times, that however much we have learned, and however many illusions, lies or misunderstandings we may have peeled away, there are still more veils and layers of clouds to be removed, and there is still a refinement, at the least, of our awareness that can be made.

When we stop reflecting, stop questioning, stop examining life, then we are in all likelihood, functionally brain dead. Stay alive. Keep asking questions, and be careful not to make assumptions, or presume that we have all the answers, or that our views are without fault or error.

7. Guilt by association

Because we tend to think in terms of either/or polarities and dichotomies of the mind – in terms of black and white, this or that – once we identify ourselves with this certain camp, we tend to shun all association with that opposite camp, as we perceive it in our minds. When this happens, even the most otherwise intelligent individuals then fall into a state of infantile befuddlement, simply due to an overly dichotomized and black and white way of thinking.

If we are on the left, we tend, for example, to be extremely reluctant, and unconsciously so, to embrace a position of being in favour of an armed citizenry, capable, at least potentially of defending itself, and with arms as a last resort, against any form of tyranny that might arise – for this would associate us with the right, and we cannot possibly have that.

I'm not of the opinion, by the way, that the right to bear arms is a critical issue, for the simple reason that I do not believe that violence for political ends is either moral or strategically intelligent. I do, however, see the argument of those who feel strongly about the issue, and I would say that the dangers posed by a government that has usurped too much power and which poses a very real threat of tyranny, far outweigh the dangers posed by any level of street crime. Weight it out, I would say, and weigh the risks. Disarming the populace is in all likelihood far more dangerous than is the mad gun culture of the United States, for example, which of course has its own costs. My point here however, is not this single issue, but what it reveals in terms of our phobia of being associated with "the other side." Such phobias of being associated with "the wrong side" are relics of a pre-pubescent mode of thinking, and are not fit for mature men and women, possessed of a basic common sense.

If we are on the right, we will be extremely hesitant, and unconsciously so, to admit that open borders are consistent with an open and free society, and that closed borders are the hallmark of totalitarian and closed societies; for this would associate us with the left, and that would be tantamount to treason in our enfeebled, cookie-cutter minds.

If you value freedom, then you value open borders. If you don't want open borders and freedom of travel, then find a nice Stalinist country to live in.

If we are fairly middle-of-the-road in our thinking and views, we will likely be loath to be associated with a number of groups. We will, for example, be unconsciously driven to avoid preparing for possible disasters – that would make us "survivalists," and we would have to be crazy, wild-eyed, paranoid Chicken Littles to be part of *that* group.

But then disaster does strike. When hurricane Katrina hit, not only were the federal government, the state and the city of New Orleans completely unprepared – *disastrously unprepared* – but so too were most of the people. Being unprepared for disaster means your ass is hanging in the wind. It is unwise, and we should correct our error now.

Katrina proved beyond all doubt that counting on the government for help in times of trouble, danger or need, is a recipe for disaster and great suffering. The people must prepare themselves, and be prepared to help one another through any and all disasters or difficult times. Prudence is precaution, and precaution is simply common sense – or moreover, basic sanity.

With the current state of the world, with economic crises and instability, political unrest, social strife and ecological crises mounting, to take a deer-in-the-headlights approach and bury our heads in the sand, or worse, to imagine that some heroic saviour figure in government or elsewhere is going to save us and protect us, is not only foolish and deeply unwise: it is by now demonstrably insane.

In the past, societies, communities and families prepared for the possibility of hard times, and the present is no different, except that the need for pre-paredness is even greater.

In the Inca civilization, as with other examples, the rule of prudence dictated that enough food would be stored to feed the entire society for at least a year, if not several years. Today it makes sense for every household, family and community to have food stocks and water on hand, as well as solar and wind power generators, seeds and medical supplies, just in case of emergency. When you get into your car, you don't think, "Today I'm going to have a car accident" – but you put your seatbelt on, just in case. It is a matter of com-mon sense. The same is true for a more general emergency preparedness.

When we are prepared, not only can we help ourselves and our families, and weather the storm far better than if we were unprepared, but we can also help others. Prepare for the worst; aim for the best. That is, or should be, common sense. And let us shun all fears of being associated with "survivalists" or any other frowned upon group. Be yourself, forget the herd, and follow your own inner wisdom and your own judgment.

Not only do we fear being associated with certain groups that we view as "others;" not only do we tend to avoid association with such groups and such people physically and in our daily life as well as our political life; and not only do we shun being thought of as a part of such groups of "others," and go out of our way, unconsciously, to avoid being labelled through guilt by asso-ciation; but we also tend to shun any views or writings from groups that are perceived as "other." This is a dangerous, self-limiting foolishness.

In certain social groups, if you are seen reading Milton Friedman or Hayek, then you get a smile and a nod of approval, and a virtual pat on the back, but if you're seen carrying a copy of the Communist Manifesto, or a little less terrifying, writings of Kropotkin, Bookchin, Bakunin or Chomsky, then you will tend to find that that smile turns to a cold look of mistrust, suspicion or disdain. In other groups, if you have a copy of the Village Voice, Mother Jones or The Nation, you get a warm smile and a nod, but if you're caught watching, or even mention that you have watched Alex Jones or a speech by Ron Paul, well, you'd better get a blanket and a cardigan, because the air is likely to become decidedly more chilly, and the look of grave doubt or suspicion is bound to come along in very short order.

But what nonsense is this? Are we men and women, or are we sheep? Must we read only one thing, or from one narrow group of individuals only? Are we modern or medieval? I think of the statement by the brilliant Irish philosopher, George Berkeley, when he said,

"When a schoolman tells me "Aristotle has said it," all I conceive he means by it is to dispose me to embrace his opinion with the deference and submission which custom has annexed to that name. And this effect is often so instantly produced in the minds of those who are accustomed to resign their judgment to the authority of that philosopher, as it is impossible any idea either of his person, writings, or reputation should go before."

I think Doug Casey is right when he says that we suffer from a medieval serf mentality. And it is not only a learned helplessness, dependency, servility, fawning deference toward power, and an illusory sense of powerlessness that haunts and paralyzes us, but also our parochial and xenophobic tribalism, in which we fear the other and cling in quiet desperation to the false comfort and security of our perceived clan.

"We are the hollow men
We are the stuffed men
Leaning together
Headpiece filled with straw. Alas!
Our dried voices, when
We whisper together
Are quiet and meaningless
As wind in dry grass

Or rats' feet over broken glass
In our dry cellar"

– *T.S. Eliot*

To artificially narrow our range of reading, or the scope of ideas and views we expose ourselves to, is as useless and self-defeating as a partial lobotomy, and in most cases, just as mind-numbing. Let our reading be broad, and our discussion and thought range freely; then, after considering a number of views and perspectives, and taking in information from a wide field, let us decide for ourselves what makes the most sense. And if we are honest and intelligent, we will have to admit that we have synthesized ideas and information from a number of sources, since no one person or group has all the answers, or the totality of the truth.

Such overly simplistic either/or thinking, which is entailed with these pervasive, subconscious ideas of guilt-by-association, blinds us in many ways, and in very serious ways, and makes our minds as dense and obscured as stone. The belief that our group is right and that we must shun all association with any other group, is simply foolish; but it is common place, and we must admit it – it exists on the right and also the left, and it is a form of ordinary madness. This too can and must be overcome, or at least guarded against and minimized. Where is our self-dignity, our self-confidence, our basic clarity of mind? We are too noble of nature and too blessed with a God-given natural intelligence and common sense for such patent absurdities and childishness.

8. Us and them thinking

We tend to think in terms of us and them. This is the single greatest downfall and weakness of human beings. We are all one family, and we are all inter-dependent and intertwined. No man is an island. Yet we tend routinely and habitually to fall into us and them thinking. It may be along the lines of race, or gender, or religion, or political ideology or affiliation, class or culture of origin, but few are free from this terrible pattern of confusion in the mind, and it does blind us severely. "We" – the good guys, the virtuous ones, the ones who know what is going on – we are right, and they are wrong – or stupid, or corrupt, or brainwashed, or ignorant, etc, etc....

Such simplistic notions must cease, and we must be on guard for them, and overcome them, whenever and wherever they arise. And the imaginary line between right and left is one of those fantasies which must be destroyed. Yes, there are very real differences of opinions and views between right and left, but we still share a common humanity, and truth be told, there is more common ground than we imagine. We must find it, or we cannot unite the people: and if we cannot unite the people, then the corporate oligarchs will win, and everyone, and also democracy and freedom, will lose.

Us and them thinking blinds us. We must rise above it. That does not mean that we all nod in agreement and have no capacity for rational thought or discourse – shudder at the thought. It does not mean that we agree on everything at all times, which would be a horror. It means simply that we recognize an underlying kinship as well as an interdependence among human beings and all living beings, in spite of our differences, and furthermore, that we can learn from each other, help one another, and find common ground in order to get some basically positive things accomplished in this world, and not be hamstrung by a division in our minds which manifests as an outward division which impales us on a spear of ignorance and vacates our power for real change.

Blind spots we all have, errors we all make, and we are not omniscient, nor infallible. To admit humbly that we are imperfect in our understanding, and yet to have the self-dignity and the confidence to bravely explore the truth ever further, is to be alive, vital and real, and to bring forth our best. That is something that we can all do, and the effort will be rewarded greatly.

JTR
February 2012

FUNDAMENTALISM AND RELATIVISM, ZEALOTRY AND OBEDIENCE:
THE SANITY BETWEEN THE TWO EXTREMES

THERE ARE MANY FORMS of fundamentalism in the world. There are religious fundamentalists of course, and there are anti-religious fundamentalists, along with political and economic fundamentalists, and others of similarly blinkered minds. Whether their ideology is religious or secular, whether they are Taliban fundamentalists or Christian fundamentalists, atheist fundamentalists, Marxist zealots or neoliberal fundamentalists, what they all share in common is their death-grip clinging to their own ideas and ideology.

There are pseudo-scientific fundamentalists who are as militant and dogmatic in their biological reductionism or epiphenomenalism as any of the medieval schoolmen were in their pet ideologies. There are also nihilists: those who pretend to be philosophical, and who are in truth the most rabid of ideologues and dogmatic militants you would ever want to meet – or not want to meet. These are known as post-modernists, which is a resurrection of the shameless ancient Greek school of Sophism, and they are adamant that there is no truth, value or meaning in the world – this is their doctrine, their creed, their dogma, their ideology, and they are deeply entrenched in it, to the point that any kind of truly philosophical or even rational conversation or dialogue is virtually impossible.

The one thing all fundamentalists have in common is a fierce and fearful, almost rabid and paranoid clinging to their ideology. A wise observer once remarked that the problem with the West is its fixation on ideology. We are enamoured, in love with our symbols and our ideas. But what is the taste of sweetness? How can you describe sweetness to someone who has never experienced it, through mere words or ideas? You cannot – words and concepts fail utterly; but one drop of honey on your tongue, and you know what sweetness is. But this is just the beginning of a process of untangling ourselves from a snare of excessive clinging to words, concepts, ideas and ideologies.

The main points to consider that come immediately to mind are these. First of all, no ideology, theology, concept, theory, paradigm or idea can possibly express or contain all of the subtleties and nuances of life, nor even the essence of it. Both in terms of subtleties and variations, and also in terms of the essential truth of the nature of being, words and concepts fail completely.

Secondly, when we cling too tightly to our ideas, ideology, theology or pet theories, we are really blinding ourselves, for we are precluding a fresh look at what is, and therefore, we have ended our learning and our gathering or refining of knowledge and understanding at a pleasant little cul de sac that we have decided to call home. Better to live in a sewer than to sink to such opacity of mind.

Thirdly, the totality of truth cannot be expressed in any one theory or ideology, no matter how badly we desire it to be so. Again, to cling too tightly to our own pet theory or beloved ideology is to put up walls to the truth and to actual seeing.

In other words, ideologues make themselves into idiots, without knowing it. This does not mean that we cannot have ideas, that we cannot draw at least tentative conclusions, or even that we cannot have strong conviction and confidence in our views: it simply means that at all times we hold our views with a little lightness, so that we may see things afresh at every moment, and not be blinded by our own filters and lenses of mind that are provided by our conceptual framework of presumed truth.

Fourth, when we clinging too tightly to our ideology, we are prone to becoming sectarian. By this I mean that, if we cling too tightly to our views, ideas or ideology, then we make ourselves sectarians in the sense that we believe only we or our club has the truth, and everybody else is either wrong or lying. Sectarianism is a very divisive and also potentially dangerous force, as we have seen in numerous religious conflicts, and also numerous ideological battles.

Again, we do not want to go so far as to paint ourselves into a corner, as the post-modernists have done, whereby we say that everybody is right, and there is no truth – the people who believe the world is flat are right, and so too are the people who believe the world is round. Insanity lies along the path of this asinine and anti-intellectual, absolutely incoherent and spineless pathology of the mind that is called nihilism, alternately known as Sophism or Post-Modernism. If we cannot draw at least tentative conclusions, say, that the earth is round, and slavery and empire are unethical and abominable to humanity, then we are either sheer cowards, snivelling cronies, or else simply mad.

The definition of fundamentalism could be said to be this, from what I have seen: 1. A deep and persistent clinging to one's ideas, concepts, theories, theology or ideology, be they secular or religious – evidence, experience and reason be damned; and 2. a narrow-minded, closed-minded, arrogant, presumptive, militant and dogmatic sectarianism that presumes that this individual or group has the only valid and correct view, and holds the entirety of the truth on the matter – a sectarianism which arises from the excessive clutching at ideas.

We need to find or rediscover the basic sanity and common sense of a middle way between the extremes of nihilistic, shoulder-shrugging relativism – which, by the way, thanks to the indirect effects of the post-modernist "movement" has become widespread and pervasive – and the bible-thumping, fist-pounding, bigoted and inane ideological zealotry which is still likewise pervasive in contemporary human society in both secular and religious terms. The way to know if you've fallen into la-la land on either extreme, either of wishy-washy, vacant relativism, or mouth-foaming ideological fixation, is to check whether A) you still believe anything with conviction, and are willing to state it aloud and live by it to the best of your ability, and B) whether you can still listen and consider other views and opinions. If you answered yes to both questions, and did so honestly, then congratulations, you are among the reasonably sane. For the rest, we may have some work to do. And, yes, it does matter.

Remember, either aggression or passivity will lead to evil. The Nazis are a prime example of militant, rabid fundamentalist fixation on an ideology. They were a horror and great threat to humanity, as all sane persons know. They were defeated because we decided not to say, 'Well, Hitler and the Nazis are just doing their own thing – who am I to judge'? The evil that was Nazism was defeated because we refused to take a passive stance. When we are rightfully wary of ideologies and strong passions, let us also remember this: "Evil can flourish in the world only when good men do nothing."

We are presently schizoid, and alternate between an avoidance of both extremes that leaves us often paralyzed in self-doubt. We do not want to be ideologues or chauvinists in any way, and pluralism is all the rage, with some justification no doubt, but we tend either to fall toward a vacant passivity of apathy or unconscious relativism, or else into an unadmitted ideological fundamentalism, or both, at different times and for different, largely unconscious motives. We must stop this now. Trust yourself, think for yourself, question everything and everyone, don't be afraid to draw conclusions or hold views, values or beliefs, or to speak them, live by them, and act upon them; and also do not forget to listen, that while we may have good reason to have confidence in our views of the earth being round or imperialism being wrong, that does not mean our understanding is perfect or our knowledge is infallible.

We need both passion and reason. That is, we need a clarity of mind and also a strong energy that is directed towards effective speech and action. Being tepid and lukewarm about everything is not always the best way. Being emotionally cool and self-contained is not always best. When it came time to abolish slavery – meaning, when the people began, finally, to admit that this abomination should never have existed, and must be abolished – there was a need for clarity of mind, and also a ferocity of speech. You do not mince words with slavers, nor do you mince words when it comes to justice or the well-being of human beings and other living beings on this earth. You speak clearly and with power to undo every injustice, as best you understand it, and to sow peace and harmony and well-being for all, even while you are aware that you are far from omniscient, and that you are not perfect in your knowledge or understanding, or even in your words or your actions. You must speak and act nonetheless, for to do otherwise is simply evil: it is an ethical error made by omission, rather than commission, and these can be nearly as great as any crime actively committed. We cannot afford, ethically or practically, to be neutral, to be passive, to be silent, or to be mealy-mouthed or weak-kneed.

Action is called for, clear and effective speech is necessary, and we bring our best forward into these demands of life upon life, or we are cowards and sheep, and should hide our faces from the sun, and walk away until we can find our courage and our inner strength.

We must beware clinging too tightly to any ideology, theory or view, for that makes us narrow, myopic and often blind. And we must also avoid the opposite extreme, of passive acceptance of what we know to be wrong or unethical, even when it is in our face and is intolerable. The Nazis represent one extreme, the extreme of the extremists who are the rabid fundamentalist ideologues. The Sophists, nihilists, relativists and post-modernists represent the other, equally insane and dangerous extreme of passivity and feeble-mindedness in the face of evil. Between these two shoals we must steer our course. There lies the middle way, and there lies basic sanity, and also the hope for the world.

While this short meditation began with the subject of fundamentalism, it must end with a focus on its opposite pole: that of passivity and silence. It would appear that the majority of people have become both passive and silent, and in fact, have been so for a long time. This is beginning to change, and change rapidly, as people are finding their voices and their courage, but there is work yet to be done.

There are the fundamentalists of the liberal centre, who may be the most zealous of all in their ideological fixation: their ideology is the ideology of not rocking the boat, not speaking too loud or out of turn, not taking a strong stance on anything, and generally, to be nice and to fit in, whatever may be happening. Even when they honestly believe themselves to be independent-minded and critical thinkers, their criticisms of the ruling order amount to the critique of the window dressings, and never the foundations. It would be like making an issue out of the chaffing of the leg irons and shackles on slaves, without ever venturing to criticize the institution of slavery itself. Such 'independent-mindedness' and 'critical thought' really merits no such terms. This is weak willed and weak minded, as well as moral cowardice, and it is unconscionable, as Martin Luther King Jr. pointed out some decades ago, and as is still the case. We have people in the centre who are happy to say that George Bush was an abominable president, that wars in the Middle East are wrong and should be ended, that civil liberties should be protected and that democracy is a fundamental value to be preserved. But when encountering a president who is even worse in foreign policy than Bush, has continued to allow the undermining of civil liberties as well as the attack on democracy, the liberal centre can only meekly ask, 'what went wrong?' – and is incapable of recognizing the obvious facts, which the majority of people now know, and which are that the business and financial elite control both major political parties in the U.S., and that the institution of corporate rule must be challenged and abolished and immediately so. But as in the former example of the chaffing of leg irons and the institution of slavery, this seems far too much to ask.

Under a Maoist or Stalinist regime, the wishy-washy centre adopts the reigning party line, and refuses to question that party line or the system that rules them. Under a Mussolini or Pinochet, the party line and structure of power is slightly different, although basically the same as under Stalinism or corporatism, and they move like limp leaf lettuce to embrace it – or at least, refuse to speak meaningfully against it. Under feudalism, theocracy or military dictatorship, the response is the same: lay low, keep quiet, try to fit in, follow the herd, don't rock the boat. Just follow the leader and do what you're told, think what you're told to think, and don't ever, ever question anything in any serious depth. In a word, obey – like a nice little poodle.

This kind of fanatical, hard-core passivity, the clinging to the unconscious ideology of powerlessness, obedience, conformity and despair, is perhaps the most dangerous thing in the world, for *it is only the passivity of the many that allows the few to do truly evil things*: it was only the passivity and silence of many that allowed the nightmare of Nazism to arise – and it was only a fierce and decidedly non-passive response to the Nazis which finally defeated that indescribable evil. The same holds true today, and the dangers, although many still do not yet realize it, are as great. (See Erich Fromm, *Escape From Freedom*.)

The vague and mild-mannered centre tends above all to want its comfort preserved – no matter the cost. If that means being silent while slavery, feudalism, Stalinism, fascism or corporatism rules, and human rights, democracy and liberty are crushed, along with the well-being and lives of others, well, that is lamentable, but not something we can afford to get our feathers ruffled about, not something to make a fuss over, and certainly not something we would wish to risk our precious little comfort and illusory security over by speaking out. This is a diabolical paralysis of the soul, and it speaks well to our lesser nature. This is how tyranny and evil arise: not because of a few bad men, but because millions of good, but complacent and timid men and women allow it.

Jesus, the Buddha and all of the great leaders of humanity have urged us to question and challenge the social order in which we find ourselves, and to throw off the mind-forged manacles of our social conditioning in order that our compassion and dignity may shine forth; but still today, many wish to live a while longer as the hollow men, in the wasteland of vacant stares and speechless open mouths – and all of us suffer for it. And yes, truth is more important than comfort, so if the truth is discomforting, that is unfortunate, but it cannot be helped. It is too late an hour and too many lives are at stake for a mincing of words now.

As Einstein said, "The world is a dangerous place. Not because of those who do terrible things. But because of those who let them do it."

Due to the pathological effects of the delusional ideology which is relativistic post-modernism, and more centrally, due to a weariness and diminished confidence, a majority of the people remain by and large passive and silent, while the world races towards a very dark time, while democracy, civil liberties, freedom and human rights are under attack, and while we continue hell bent towards ecological self-annihilation. We must now regain our basic dignity, confidence, and self-trust, embrace our power and our voice, and stand up for what we believe, before there is nothing left to stand for, nor any ground to stand upon. And it is both for others' future and also our own: this is our world too, our life, and we should embrace it, while we are here, and not squander it.

We all have common sense, and a natural intelligence is native to all human beings. We can and should, and must trust that now, or the tiny minority that are ideological fundamentalists, empire mongers and obsessively driven by vanity and greed, will destroy all possibility of a future for us all.

The common sense of the people will save us, but only if the people acknowledge and bring forth, and above all, trust in their own common sense. Without this, we are lost, for the majority will continue to behave as meek and obedient sheep, while the ravenous, the predatory, the insatiable and the megalomaniacal destroy all freedom, democracy, justice, peace, and all future for humanity. Stop this. Trust yourself.

Again, as Oscar Wilde said, "Disobedience, in the eyes of anyone who has read history, is man's original virtue." Trust yourself.

Your common sense is more valuable than all of the reams of verbiage and papers produced by the technocrats and the pundits, and the empire-frenzied madmen whom they serve. Stand now, or watch the world die. Yes, it has become that stark. There is no more time for delay.

JTR
November 15, 2011

ORDER AND CHAOS:
THE END OF CORPORATE NEO-FEUDALISM
AND THE BIRTH OF REAL DEMOCRACY

A WORLD ORDER IS DYING, a new world is being born – there will be tremors. A little chaos now is exactly what we need – that is, a disruption of the existing "order" that is killing us slowly, and with increasing speed.

The majority of people are by nature conservative, and that is, philosophically and in their disposition, and not in political ideology – that is, most people are wary of change, and tend to prefer the familiar norm, no matter how pathological, devilish, destructive or mad the norm may have become: but this is a general disposition, and there are decisive moments in human history when the great majority of the people become fed up with the norm of their time, and throw it off, like chaff in the wind – the detritus of the past, shackles cast to the ground, or a heavy weight no longer wanted or needed. This is one of those times.

The currently ruling social order has become a kind of global neo-feudalism, in which an international corporate elite now dominate both the economy and also the political process, by way of essentially buying the allegiance of their servants who are the political elite. The business elite thus now rules in all but name – just as King George of England ruled an empire two hundred years ago, and just as the aristocracy ruled in earlier feudal times – while the military and political elite serve them. The people now know and recognize the fact that there has been a silent corporate coup or takeover of our democracy and our society: and this norm the people are beginning to reject, as they should, and rightfully so, and as they must.

> *"Lethargy, the forerunner of death to the public liberty...."*
> *"The spirit of resistance to government is so valuable on certain occasions,*
> *that I wish it to be always kept alive...."*
> *"I hold it, that a little rebellion, now and then, is a good thing, and as*
> *necessary in the political world as storms in the physical."*
>
> *– Thomas Jefferson*

The present order is anything but orderly: it is sowing destruction both economically and also ecologically and socially, it is lawless and anti-democratic, fundamentally at odds with justice, with basic decency, with human rights, with economic, social or ecological stability and security, with peace, and with basic sanity and common sense. This present order is leading us straight into, not anarchy, but chaos and tyranny. This has to be stopped so that a sane and just order can emerge from the rubble of this collapsing regime. And this is what is happening now.

In order for chaos to be avoided, a little chaos is needed – that is, in order to end this current corrupt and anti-democratic, unjust and ecologically suicidal order, an order which is driving us with ever greater speed toward the chaos of ecological cataclysm and ruin, as well as destitution and subjugation under a neo-feudal empire, a change is needed, and that change will entail a little chaos as the old order dies and a new and more just and democratic order is born.

Clinging to the present norm and the established order and regime will only harm us now. We must embrace change – and real change, not mere rhetoric – in order for humanity to live in justice, freedom, democracy and peace, and in order for humanity to simply survive, as well as to thrive. Change – real change – is coming, is arising now, as we speak, and change we must not fear, but embrace now, and even urge and demand.

I think it's time for a little chaos to break up the orderly chaos: the present and long-standing "order" of pseudo-democracy and corporate rule is killing us and the planet, destroying any chance for a future for humanity. In the ever-existing balance between order and chaos, we can fall too far to one side, and when we do, life is degraded, if not destroyed, and this is the case if we lean too far in either direction: toward a chaotic disregard for order, or toward a life-destroying obedience to a current, established order.

Presently, leaning too far toward a preference for order, and a fear of chaos or disruption of the existing order, is frankly suicidal, and also grossly unethical, as well as naive, profoundly unwise, and a sign of wilful ignorance if not simple corruption.

Change is needed, and urgently so: the passive and the complicit and the defenders of the reigning order will have to be moved aside, or else brought aboard the movement for real and positive social change. Fortunately, such a movement for real change has emerged, and is building rapidly.

As always, there are early adopters, pioneers, leaders – and also foot-draggers, the obstinate, the calcified of heart and mind, the stubborn and intractable ideologues, and the brutally, wilfully ignorant or deeply cynical who resist the changes that are undeniably needed. A couple of quotes from Thoreau express the difficulty of creating positive change, and are relevant here.

> "The mass of men lead lives of quiet desperation... But it is a characteristic of wisdom not to do desperate things."

> "When we consider what, to use the words of the catechism, is the chief end of man, and what are the true necessaries and means of life, it appears as if men had deliberately chosen the common mode of living because they preferred it to any other. Yet they honestly think there is no choice left. But alert and healthy natures remember that the sun rose clear. It is never too late to give up our prejudices. No way of thinking or doing, however ancient, can be trusted without proof. What everybody echoes or in silence passes by as true today may turn out to be falsehood tomorrow, mere smoke of opinion, which some had trusted for a cloud that would sprinkle

fertilizing rain on their fields. What old people say you cannot do, you try and find that you can."

"When I observe the ruts in a road, I am compelled to think, how much deeper the ruts of the mind?"

"I sometimes despair of getting anything done with the help of my fellow men. Their minds would first have to be placed in a sort of powerful vice, to squeeze their old ideas out of them."

Again, fortunately, life has squeezed them, or more to the point, the reigning corporate elite, in their greed and hubris, have squeezed the people to the breaking point, to the point where they naturally are nudged or drawn into a period of deep reflection, re-assessment, and frankly, revolution. This is exactly what we need now: reflection, re-assessment, and democratic revolution.

The imperial hubris of the reigning elite, like all other would-be god-kings and emperors before them, has brought forth the seeds of their downfall and dethronement – and none too soon, for we are racing toward a cliff of ecological self-annihilation from which we cannot recover if we allow ourselves to go over, and which we will go over unless this current global corporatist order is questioned, challenged, and overturned in favour of democracy, justice, peace and ecological sanity. It is not too late, but we are fast running out of time. As Martin Luther King said, there is a time when we must face the fierce urgency of now.

"We are now faced with the fact, my friends, that tomorrow is today. We are confronted with the fierce urgency of now. In this unfolding conundrum of life and history, there is such a thing as being too late. Procrastination is still the thief of time. Life often leaves us standing bare, naked, and dejected with a lost opportunity. The tide in the affairs of men does not remain at flood – it ebbs. We may cry out desperately for time to pause in her passage, but time is adamant to every plea and rushes on. Over the bleached bones and jumbled residues of numerous civilizations are written the pathetic words, "Too late." There is an invisible book of life that faithfully records our vigilance or our neglect."

– Martin Luther King Jr.

"The era of procrastination, of half-measures, of soothing and baffling expedients, of delays, is coming to its close. In its place we are entering a period of consequences."

– Winston Churchill

There are times to move slowly, times to proceed with caution, times to take a long time to decide upon a course of action, times to wait and see what unfolds or to gather further evidence before drawing any conclusions or acting in any way other than what is routine. Now is not such a time. The evidence is clear, the urgency is obvious and fierce. The pressures are mounting, and disaster is looming. We must act now, and decisively, to restore democracy to the people, to reclaim democracy in the hands of the people, to reverse the corporate coup which has paralyzed and hijacked our democracy, and to end this madness of systemic injustice and global ecocide before we end humanity and destroy our future altogether. The time is now. It is time for action. It is time for democracy. It is time for a second wave of democratic revolutions. And this is just what is arising now, at long last, and none too soon.

Allowing the present order of global neo-feudal corporatism to continue is not acceptable to any thinking human being today. It must change, and this order must end. A new order must be created, and in the transition, there will be the break-up of the old order, which by necessity will entail some degree of disruption of "business as usual." This is to be expected, and should be welcomed, even embraced and championed. The old order must die for a new order to be born. Fortunately, it is dying, and a new day is on the horizon. Let us not be timid, nor seek to cling to the shadows of this dying spectre which yet haunts the world. A new day is approaching, and the bold and the brave of heart will be its heralds.

Chris Hedges put it frankly and concisely, summing up a major element of what is motivating the Occupy Wall Street movement and the emerging pro-democracy movements around the world, when he said: "reversing the corporate coup is now a matter of life and death – *it is a matter of the survival of our species. Many people have been saying this for some time, but just this*

fall, in 2011, have the people begun to awaken, not only to the situation at hand, but also to their power. The people are beginning to recognize that the current order is unjust and also self-destructive, and that it must change, and change now, in order for humanity to have a decent future, or any future at all. In that sense, a little chaos now may be our only hope of survival, for chaos means, in essence, a break-up of the existing pattern or order."

Chaos does not necessarily entail violence or mass insanity, even though the mass media use the term routinely to imply such. In its essence, chaos means simply a break-up or disruption of established orders or patterns, which precedes and makes way for new patterns to arise (see Ilya Prigogine, James Gleick, James Lovelock, Thomas Kuhn) – and a disruption of the established order is exactly what we need.

In human history, science, ecology, or natural history, there is and has always been a complementarity of opposites, a dance, an ebb and flow, a dynamic equilibrium which is not static or fixed but ever in flux, ever fluid, between order and chaos. Order is not order, but simply the repetition of established patterns – whether these are benign, malignant or neutral. Chaos is not chaos but simply the disruption of established patterns and the emergence of new patterns.

Without both continuity and change, and a dynamic and ever flowing, ever changing equilibrium between continuity and change, no life would be possible. That is to say, without both "order" and "chaos," no life would be possible. And when the current order unduly constricts or threatens life, then a little chaos is needed in order to renew life and allow it to continue to breathe and thrive again.

When an established pattern or "order" begins to fall apart, break down, collapse or shift to a new and emerging pattern, it may appear to be chaos, and in some sense, in this essential and unbiased sense, it is: it is a break-up of the existing order or pattern, and the emergence of a new order or pattern. Human beings tend to lean toward one pole or the other, with the great majority preferring stability, continuity and familiarity – that is, "order" – over what they perceive as chaos, but which in reality is simply creative flux or change. Those fearful of change are fearful of a loss of the established order, or even a loss of order per se and completely. They have no understanding of life. Life is always with flux, and change is the one eternal. Old orders and patterns are forever dying, while new patterns and orders are forever being born. To cling to either chaos or order is to miss the point entirely, and to fail to see or understand the nature of life.

When the ancient regime of feudalism was being challenged and was crumbling during the American and French Revolutions, the supporters of the old order saw the popular uprisings as chaos, as a breakdown of "order" and as a threat. Of course, the revolutionaries saw the old order as a diseased and oppressive state of society, and perceived its continuation as a threat to the well-being and aspirations of humanity. One side saw the old order as order per se, to be defended to the death, viewing the social turmoil and discontent, the revolutionary spirit, as chaos and disruption without redemption or value. The other side saw the old order as oppressive and outmoded, and saw the revolutionary disruption of the old order as necessary and healthy, a sign of great hope for humanity. Of course, two hundred years later, the vast majority of people would now side with the revolutionaries, and say that the old order was indeed oppressive and was limiting and thwarting human potential, and was rightly overturned – that is, today we look back and say that that time of chaos was needed and essential to the flowering of human society in a fuller, richer, more just and noble form. Few today would say that we should return to feudalism, or that the revolutionary "chaos" or disruption of the old order was wrong, unethical or unproductive. Two hundred years from now, people will look back and view the break-up of our current world order of global neo-feudal corporatism, through a second wave of democratic revolutions, as absolutely essential – not only to the full flowering of democracy, justice and human potential, but to the very survival of the species.

Change requires change, and not mere rhetoric for purposes of getting elected to some high office – and change involves the disruption of the old order. If you wish to preserve the old order, you cannot simultaneously speak meaningfully of change, nor work towards it. Lech Walesa could not speak of change and simultaneously support the Communist Party or the Soviet empire. Nelson Mandela could not speak of change and simultaneously support the apartheid regime. Gandhi could not speak of change and simultaneously uphold the foreign rule of the British Empire. Martin Luther King could not speak of change and at the same time defend the institutions of racism, militarism, classism and empire. These true leaders spoke of change, and understood that change would mean a disruption of the old order; and they welcomed and embraced, and encouraged just such a disruption, for they sought a new and better order for humanity, which required the death of the old order. Advocating real change means advocating a break from the existing and established order or pattern of the present. Anything other is simple deceit, or else madness and self-delusion. Certain dubious politicians spring to mind, but that is an aside, and they are by now quite irrelevant in any case.

The important point is that change requires change, and change requires a disruption of the norm. And usually, when change emerges within human societies, positive change at least, it is because human beings have begun to recognize that, as Erich Fromm expressed it, the norm has become a profoundly abnormal norm – that is, the norm has become in some ways pathological or unwholesome, and must be overturned and replaced by a new and more sane and humane norm.

When slavery was resisted and the abolition movement started to gain momentum, many saw it as a threat to order, and saw it as disruption and chaos without value or redeeming qualities. Of course, they were wrong: the old order which endowed slavery with moral, cultural and legal sanction and justification was evil, and was rightfully overturned. Overturning an injustice, as Jesus overturned the tables of the money changers in the temple, may look like chaos in the moment, and may entail a degree of chaos, in the proper sense, the root sense, which is a disruption of an established or long-standing order or pattern, but it is a necessary chaos that is creative and opens new possibilities for fullness, dignity and richness of life for human beings. In other words, chaos can be, and often is and has been, a creative force, and is not necessarily a destructive force.

Creative chaos was exemplified by Jesus throwing the money changers from the temple, or his challenging of the religious and social hierarchies and vested interests of the day. It was exemplified by the abolitionists overturning and ending slavery. It was exemplified by the suffragettes who sought and won an end to the male-dominated practices and cultural norms which prevented women the natural and inalienable right to vote. Creative chaos can be seen in the speeches of Martin Luther King Jr. and in the brave actions of millions of people who participated in the civil rights and peace movements. It can be seen in the democratic revolutionaries of two hundred years ago. And it can be seen in the men and women who are standing up now, speaking out now, and becoming a part of the second wave of democratic revolutions, which are just now beginning around the world – though most do not yet recognize it, and many unwisely and heedlessly fear it.

Destructive chaos is exemplified in the existing "order" under which we live, and which every day threatens our lives and our children's lives, for it threatens our very existence on this planet, and not only our dignity, well-being, freedom and democracy. The existing order is an on-going destructive chaos, at the same time that it is an entrenched and established "order" or system of self-replicating patterns. And the stark truth is this: if this destructive chaos of the existing order is left unchecked and is allowed to continue, not only will democracy and freedom cease to exist, but human beings will also cease to exist on this planet. It has come to that point. The present order is not only unjust, anti-democratic, inhumane, brutal, oppressive, banal and obscene, but also suicidal. It is a pattern or order which must end.

For one order to end and another to begin, there must be, of necessity, a period of disruption of the old order. This is both logically obvious upon reflection, and also historically demonstrable and abundantly clear. You cannot have the end of one order and the beginning of another without some degree of disruption, that is, a certain degree of creative chaos, unless of course you live in Oz.

But we do not live in Oz. We live on the earth, and here on earth, the break-up of old orders and the establishment of new orders, comes with at least some degree of disruption and creative chaos. This is to be expected, this is natural, this is unavoidable, and this is entirely necessary. Let us make no mistake about it.

When the present global order of neo-feudal corporatism falls, as it will, and it is crumbling now, there will be some degree or measure of chaos or disruption in its disintegration. It cannot be helped. There will be a time of transition, and hopefully it will be, on the whole, a remarkably peaceful transition. But there will of necessity be disruption, if for no other reason, than for the simple reason that the old "order" is dying, and is falling apart. Be brave. A new world is being born. And that world will embrace freedom and democracy – it must, for by now that is the only world that is at all viable.

As an additional component to the mix or flux that is arising now, we can say with certainty that the presently ruling corporate elite are not likely to want to cede power voluntarily, or to make way for authentic democracy and the reclaiming by the people their rightful democratic power. On the contrary, the currently ruling oligarchical and plutocratic corporate elite are likely to try to hold onto their power, and to prop up the now dying and crumbling old order. It is a failing and failed strategy, as history has shown, for every empire that has ever arisen has also fallen, but the mad men who love power more than life will likely repeat the errors of history once more, imperial hubris pushing them in patterns of infantile grandiosity to achieve what no emperor has ever achieved, which is lasting power and domination. Their attempts to hold onto power may be violent, and may bring in an added element of chaos which might otherwise have been avoided. It is not too late for a peaceful transition to authentic democracy and an end to the currently reigning corporatist regime of neo-feudalism, but the ruling elite may thwart any attempt to create a positive change for humanity, and thwart it with a fierce and violent stubbornness in the face of the rising other superpower, which is humanity itself. Let us hope that they are not quite as mad and as depraved as that, but they may well be.

The other element of chaos which may be added to the mix as the old order dies and a new order is born, is the destructive chaos that can be unleashed in times of a break-down of old orders. Sometimes old orders die peacefully, as they did when the Soviet bloc collapsed between 1989 and 1991. Only in Romania was there limited violence, and that was on the part of the old guard that was trying to protect the dying regime. Everywhere else, the Soviet empire collapsed with remarkable peacefulness. It fell in upon itself like a house of cards, and violence was rare during the fall of the old regime. Elsewhere, in other times, we have not been so fortunate, or so wise. During the French Revolution, there arose such a furor of hatred and fear that a very dark period, The Terror, arose, for a short but terrible time. What we can see from these two examples, without even mentioning others, is that there is a natural and inevitable element of chaos entailed in all major social change, revolution or break-up of old orders, but the time of change or transition, the time of revolution and its aftermath, can be anything from remarkably peaceful, to horrifically violent and brutal. In other words, chaos is inevitable and necessary for any change, but creative chaos is based in love and boldness of vision, while destructive chaos is based in greed, hate and fear, and destructive chaos we should wish to avoid, if we are at all sane, even while acknowledging that creative chaos, chaos that challenges and overturns corrupt, unjust or oppressive orders, is necessary and unavoidable and much needed.

Hopefully the limited chaos or shake-up of the present established "order" will be within the parameters of basic sanity, goodwill and common sense, but in any event, a disruption and a transformation of the current order is needed, and needed urgently I would say; and I for one (along with Jefferson) trust the people far more than the reigning power elite, or any other elite. The existing order is both unjust and suicidal: it cannot continue, and must therefore be disrupted, halted, and overturned, and immediately so, before our extinction is finally guaranteed by our own inaction and drift toward oblivion.

Democracy, as Chomsky also said, is probably our only hope. We need it now, and that means a disruption of the existing plutocratic order of global neo-feudal corporatism, aka, corporate fascism, or rule by the astronomically wealthy.

As to human history, I think the anthropological evidence that came to light – quietly – in the 1970s, and which has yet to percolate through the field of anthropology much less the general populace, shows that war, conquest, inequality and empire are anything but immutable facts of human society, but rather the aberration to which we have become so accustomed as to not question it.

(See Rianne Eisler's, *The Chalice and the Blade*, and far better, Murray Bookchin's, *The Ecology of Freedom*, for more on this.)

Thankfully, people are now questioning whether these pathologies of human society really are inevitable, or whether they can, at least to a large degree, be overcome and put behind us. I believe they can, and it is clear from the longer view of history that this is a fact. Whether or not we act upon what is possible to create a better, although not utopian or perfect world, is up to us.

I can understand the scepticism of many people, but for myself, I have to focus on what is possible, and aim for the better of possible unfoldings, and work toward them. I agree with Thoreau in many ways, including this:

> *"Ultimately men hit only what they aim for, therefore,*
> *they had better aim high."*

And with Goethe, when he said,

> *"If you can imagine something, begin it. Boldness has genius within it."*

I also agree with the lucidity and common sense expressed by Chomsky when he said that the present holds ominous portent and signs of great hope – and that what ensues is largely up to us. And also when he said, again, with his usual lucid common sense: if we assume that nothing can be done and no change is possible, then we have guaranteed the outcome – but if we suspend our disbelief and hold out the possibility at least of change, then change may well become possible.

Again, the only hope we have is to try; and to not try, is to me, simply unethical, and ethically intolerable. To me, cynicism is both unethical, for it leads to passivity if not actual complicity in the face of evil; and also a living death. We must aim high, or else die slowly and with a whimper. I am not fond of either slow death or whimpering, so I for one must act. Fortunately, many people are now feeling the same. More than that, I would say a revolution has begun, and it is greatly, even urgently needed. The time of pseudo-democracy and plutocratic corporate rule must now end. Let democracy reign, and let a new day begin.

There will be a degree of disruption, an element of creative chaos as the old order is questioned, challenged, and ultimately overturned and replaced with a more authentic democracy and a more just and sane order. We should acknowledge that this is both unavoidable and also necessary, and embrace the disruption of the old order and further it, so that a greater justice and a fuller flowering of democracy may be born. If we do not, if we are timid or overly obedient, deferential or complicit, we shall fail not only ourselves and our children, but also all of humanity, and all life on earth, for this currently reigning order is rapidly destroying not only the quality of life, well-being and peace of all, the rights and freedoms of all, and the last remnants of real democracy, but also the basis of continued life on this planet.

To be silent now is to be complicit with what is, without mincing words, frankly an unjust and evil, monolithic and self-destructive order. To be actively complicit with this order is no longer excusable, if it ever was. When people after World War II said they were "just doing their jobs," the Nuremburg Trials held them responsible for their actions, and found them morally and criminally guilty of serious and grave crimes against humanity. The time is coming soon when, in not too many years, our time will be looked back upon, and the complicit and the silent will be held in contempt, if they are forgiven at all. We cannot be silent now, and we cannot be complicit or compliant with an order that has thrown humanity and all values overboard in its relentless pursuit of greed, power and megalomaniacal self-aggrandizement in the dream of a few madmen of becoming god-kings.

This madness must end, and end it will. A little chaos and disruption will be inevitable in the process, and we should not fear it. Neither should we unnecessarily exacerbate it. What will hold us strong and true, is not our commitment to "order" or even to law, for as Martin Luther King, Thoreau, Gandhi, Thomas Jefferson and others have proclaimed and have shown, when the existing order is or has become corrupt, and when laws are twisted or perverted to serve that unjust and corrupt order, and to suppress the people and to stifle justice, then it is not only the right, but yes, the obligation of the people to break ranks with that order, and if necessary to defy those laws which obstruct true justice. No, it is not a loyalty to "order" or to a certain existing order or system or structure, nor even a loyalty to the law, but as Thoreau said, and as Jesus and Jefferson and Gandhi and King each demonstrated, loyalty to the truth and to justice which must come before and above any and all loyalties to norms, laws, powers or conventions. It is not love of order or law that will aid us now or guide us wisely and well, but love of truth and love of justice. And for justice and truth to reign, a little freedom is necessary, and actually, a substantial freedom, for free speech, freedom of inquiry, freedom of thought and belief, freedom of expression, freedom of assembly and the right to rebel, resist and to revolution when the existing order becomes oppressive or stubbornly corrupt, are all necessary to both justice and the pursuit of truth.

In short, order without a little chaos becomes a tomb, and all that tomb can contain is the rotting carcass of a decaying humanity. Let that not be our fate. Inject a little life into this stolid and staid, long stagnant and overly dormant, sleep-walking society, and let truth and justice be our new guiding lights, above and over "law and order." Without truth and justice, there can be no just laws, and no sane, wise or even decent order.

All truly positive change in human society has come with and come from a creative rebellion against the existing norm, and against the reigning order of the time. Chaos, that is, is the mother of every new order. To fear chaos is to fear change, and thus to fear life, for *life is change.*

Fearing change is fearing life, as life cannot and does not exist except in a state of constant and perpetual flux. Embrace the changes that are needed, and that an awakened humanity is now pressing toward. It is time.

Those who cling to order do so because they believe that that order, so called, will provide them with security. Here is news, and sad though it may be, it is the truth: this order is slowly killing you; this order has no allegiance or loyalty to you; this order views you and all people, all life and all living beings as expendable; this order is rapidly eliminating and eviscerating the middle class, and pushing the great majority of the people into an ever-sinking underclass – and more over, most abominable and most intolerable of all, this present order is destroying the very basis of life on earth, and destroying the future of your children, and your children's children.

This order has no allegiance to you or to anyone but the ruling fraction of a percent who control it – why should you remain loyal to it, or continue to defend it? We are suffering from a pandemic condition of Stockholm syndrome – we have identified with our captors.

This present, ruling order of human society is suicidal. If you do not, or cannot, or will not, for your own sake stand up to it and declare that freedom, democracy, justice, peace and environmental sanity be placed above greed, power lust and egomania, then at the very least, stand up and speak out and demand these things for the sake of your children, for the sake of their children, and for the sake of the nearly four billion children of this earth who deserve a future, and not simply an inherited bone yard of desolation. There is no time for silence or complicity or deferential obedience to a dying and corrupt order any longer. Conscience, even basic sanity, demand that we stand now, and make a change.

Your security, the security of all peoples of this earth, now rests with our most basic and prized of treasures, whether we have realized their value prior to this moment or not, and these are: our own strength of heart, our basic common sense, and human solidarity – that is, ordinary men and women helping one another in good times and bad, standing together in common cause for a better world for all, standing in the strength of our unity across our great and wondrous diversity, and standing for a few basic and shared values that the overwhelming majority of us can and do agree upon: such as ecological sanity, peace, freedom, justice, the rights and dignity of all, and the authentic democracy that is our only means of attaining and preserving these values.

Stand now. Your security lies in the solidarity of your fellow men and women, and not in this fast-crumbling and dying regime. If you are timid, think of your children, or your grandchildren, or the children of this world: they need your action and your voice – now, and not later, when it is too late. Stand now.

For just over two hundred years, and in many nations and much less time than this, we have been living with what can best and most accurately be described as a gestational, fledgling form of democracy. Contrary to popular belief and cherished illusions, democracy did not spring fully mature from the womb, but has been an emerging process of maturation over the past decades and centuries. The American revolution, for example, enshrined democratic rights, freedoms and empowerment to all white property-owning males. It took nearly two hundred years to begin to draw forth the greater potential and fuller development of democracy, and to overcome the initial self-contradictions and errors of racism, sexism and classism. These same errors are still present, but surely all can see that we have taken democracy from one, early form, to a much fuller form, in the course of two centuries.

The democratic revolutionaries and founders of modern democracy were insightful, even prescient, but they were not omniscient, nor infallible. We have learned from their mistakes as well as their triumphs, as every genera- tion must do with regards to every preceding generation.

And while we were watching this beautiful young child, which is democ- racy, grow and mature, and as we nourished her as best we could, and sought vigilantly to protect her from harm, there were always some who secretly or openly loathed her, and wished her dead. Even while she was still young, even before she reached her full maturity, there were those who sought to strangle her in her sleep, and to return us to an earlier, more brutal and stark, feudal era, where the few reign over the many without any hindrance from such notions as democracy or the will of the people. And more to the point, and it is a fact that many people have now sadly come to realize, this precious child now has been kidnapped, held ransom, and stolen from us by the same imperial forces of hubris and greed that would have her dead, so that they may rule unencumbered by the wishes or needs or aspirations of the people.

Democracy, as virtually everybody now knows, or is rapidly coming to real- ize, has been taken hostage. These same imperial forces that wished her dead, have captured her, and made her their mistress. She became to her captors, was made to become, first a mistress, and then a concubine. And now, she is a chattel, a piece of property owned by her new masters, to be used, and to be disposed of, when the time suits her new lords. And the time is nearing when the new feudal lords shall send her off to the back chamber, to quietly have her executed, and with it, our dreams and our freedom, our future, and all hope for humanity.

This is no mere metaphor. This is precisely what has happened. We have watched, in all too much quiet and passivity, as our young and still develop- ing democracy was first dominated, and then taken captive, by a new era of robber barons, the new feudal lords, they who call themselves, quite literally and absurdly, "the masters of the universe" – the reigning corporate elite who have taken over democracy, as they have taken over the airwaves, the resources of the earth, the factories, the fields; even many of the parks and most of the commons, they have claimed as their own: and now, they have usurped our greatest treasure, which is our democracy, the power of the people to govern themselves and to choose their own destiny. This they have stolen, and before our child democracy was even fully mature.

To this theft of democracy, this abomination upon democracy, this capture and degradation and imperilment of democracy, we must and do now say, No.

Democracy was not yet fully mature nor fully developed in her greatest flowering before she had been captured by interests who wish to make her a pawn of their grand imperial ambitions. It is time to end this madness, end this injustice, and restore democracy to where she belongs, which is with the people. She is their child, and she belongs to them, and them alone. They will not tolerate her capture or abuse any further. The paralysis of fear and the illusions of powerlessness give way at last, sooner or later, to a determination that knows no limits and no end, to a resolve that is unwavering and unstoppable – and that time has come.

The presently ruling global corporate elite believe, foolishly, that they are immune from the facts and lessons of history, that their empire shall not crumble, but shall last forever, that they, unlike all emperors before them, can continue to accumulate vast wealth and power while the people suffer, and parade their power, even if it is silently and in closed doors and shadowy corridors, without the people rising up and saying 'no more' – that they can act with impunity, and are above all law, all moral restraints, and all forces of nature and history. They are wrong.

The people have awoken. Democracy shall prevail. The game is not yet over. There is at least one hand more yet to play – and the people hold all the cards, as the elite know very well. It is a showdown, between a reigning imperial global neo-feudalism of corporate rule, and authentic democracy, for the benefit of all the people, with government of the people, by the people, for the people. And democracy shall reign.

You who call yourselves masters of the universe, and you who support them, as idle servants, lapdogs, talking heads and spin doctors – the writing is on the wall. The people have awakened, and your time in power is about to end.

People of the earth, heed the call: the time for the full flowering of democracy is now. Stand now. Let your voices be heard. This is your time. Unite now, under the banner of democracy, with freedom and justice and rights for all, or watch your world wither and die in pain. The choice we face now has become that stark. Stand now.

JTR
November 3, 2011

PRE-REVOLUTIONARY FRANCE AND AMERICA:
1785 AND NOW

READING ABOUT THE FRENCH revolution, some interesting parallels came to mind: parallels with the present.

Among the primary causes of the revolution of 1789 in France: excessive, despotic powers of government, such as the ability to arrest anyone without trial or due process by law....... hmmm..... sounds familiar.

And also, financial crisis of the government: the treasury bankrupt....again, same as now with the U.S. Treasury. The U.S. debt is now over $10 trillion, annual deficits are over a trillion dollars, and the trade deficit is over $600 billion a month. India, OPEC nations and others have begun a sell-off of U.S. dollars. Even drug lords are getting out of the dollar, preferring Euros for drug money laundering. The recent $10 trillion bail-out of Wall Street only brought the U.S. Treasury, dollar and economy closer to collapse. When the dollar finally does crash, U.S. instability and popular discontent will spike. Already discontent is high and mounting.

Conditions are ripe for revolution in the U.S., as the goons in Langley have noted themselves. (The CIA apparently has predicted a greater than 50% chance of a revolution in America within the next five years.)

A third similarity between pre-revolutionary France and pre-revolutionary (present) America: the costs of empire bankrupted the government and society, leading to great political and economic instability. (See Ron Paul, senior member of the house banking and finance committee.)

The aristocracy of pre-revolutionary France tended to live in lavish indulgence, while the commoners, the peasants and ordinary workers, suffered great hardships. Meanwhile, the wealthy aristocracy were given exemptions from most taxes, while the ordinary people were taxed heavily and onerously. Again, then as now. (See "Free Lunch" on Democracy Now!)

But even within the ranks of the privileged minority, there was a huge difference between the small elite who dominated the country, and owned most of its land, and the merely privileged, who were often little better off than the average peasants, and only slightly more secure. Thus there were divisions between the minority who were merely privileged, and the truly wealthy elite few who dominated the nation and lived in lavish excess. Again, then as now.

These tensions between the privileged and the elite grew to explosive proportions: it was not just the poor that sought revolution, but much of the economically squeezed and quite insecure privileged classes. We will see what the formerly privileged middle class will do when they watch themselves fall ever further into economic insecurity and loss. Revolution comes not just from the ghettos and the slums. The middle class is being eliminated. They will not be happy with this turn of events.

With the middle class now, in 2010, highly insecure, heavily in debt, and falling into the underclass, there will be a split between the formerly privileged and the elite, as happened in 1789 in France. The results will be transformative, to put it mildly. (See *Uprising*, by David Sirota, and *Global Showdown*, by Maude Barlow.)

Pre-revolutionary France had developed a culture in which people felt they had rights and were justified in defending them. Similar now, and even more so.

Pre-revolutionary France had outlawed torture. But the regime was still held to be too despotic, and so was overthrown by the people.

Torture now is legalized, and even defended by Republicans and Democrats alike, including Obama, as necessary for security. The fuse is lit. The regime is going down.

Gore Vidal was right: America is living in pre-revolutionary times.

"France in the mid-1780's was a society afflicted with numerous tensions. Nevertheless, it was not obvious that the country was on the brink of revolutionary explosion" wrote Jeremy D. Popkin in *A Short History of the French Revolution*. Nor is it obvious to most today that conditions are ripe for just such a juncture in history. It seems that only the elite and their minions recognize the extreme instability of the Western nations (see global poll 2001 by World Economic Forum) – and they are making preparations in response, as we should as well.

Gandhi, Martin Luther King Jr., Henry David Thoreau, Thomas Jefferson, Étienne de La Boétie and many others, can help us find our way, our feet, and our voices. It is time to stand.

> *"Long-term trends had made a major crisis in France possible, but it took specific events to make it unavoidable. The most important...was the fact that by late 1786 the French government was finally on the verge of complete insolvency."*
>
> *– Jeremy D. Popkin*

Sound familiar? 10 trillion dollars. Bear that figure in mind. The people are furious, and Obama is slapping wrists, after having signed many of the cheques.

The Wall Street mob – the banking elite – just swindled the U.S. out of trillions of dollars. The result is a simmering resentment and indignation among the American people that is slowly coming to a boil – along with the effective bankruptcy of the U.S. Treasury.

You cannot go on printing money to pay your debts (or extortion money) without devaluing and ultimately collapsing the currency.

The U.S. dollar will crash, and when it does, the U.S. Treasury will be insolvent. The game will be over. Revolution will be likely within short order.

(Note that after the writing of this essay the U.S. dollar did rally somewhat against the weakening of the Euro, but this does not change the underlying structural picture of the dollar or its systemic devaluation and eventual collapse. But even before a U.S. currency collapse, the American people and people around the world are showing signs they are fed up. – Note added November 17, 2011)

The people will not take much more. You can't piss down their backs all day, day in and day out, and say it's raining, without them noticing, and understanding what is going on. (Something is trickling down. But it isn't jobs or justice, economic benefits or prosperity.)

George Soros stated in an interview with the *Atlantic Monthly*, in 2001 I believe –speaking as a member of the global business elite, to the elite – "We must make major compromises now, or we will lose everything." This is a clarion call: a clear and unequivocal statement of a profound crisis of legitimacy for the ruling order. But note the obvious: the elite do not want to compromise, nor do they want to lose all power and privilege. Only one option remains if that is their choice, as it clearly is: consolidate power while they can, before losing it. The implications should be self-evident: and they are not pleasant.

The people are just about fed up. Get ready for some interesting times. It may be a challenge, but it is also an opportunity.

A door is about to open – or has opened already. Who among us will walk through? A better day awaits.

The Wall Street barons must be dethroned. It is time to reclaim democracy.

JTR
January 26, 2010

Note that this was written a year and a half before people started to occupy Wall Street and protests spread across 1,000 cities world-wide within the following months. The essay called for the dethronement of the Wall Street barons, and predicted that the people would not take much more – that a door was about to open. It has. And this is only the beginning.

RECLAIMING DEMOCRACY FOR THE COMMON GOOD – AND FOR THE SURVIVAL AND FUTURE OF OUR CHILDREN:
THE POLITICAL ECONOMY OF ENVIRONMENTAL SANITY AND DEMOCRATIC RENEWAL

SEPTEMBER 27, 2011, THE Global Footprint Network declared as Earth Overshoot Day: the day that humans have used up all renewable resources available for the year. Not good. This obviously cannot continue. Limitless growth in material consumption and "production" clearly cannot be sustained on a finite planet. We can have limitless growth in culture, the arts, science, the mind, spirituality and quality of life, but not in material production and consumption. We are depleting our collective inheritance: which should rightfully be shared equitably, through democratic popular control of the commons to which we all share usufructory rights – despite our present unjust and unwise socio-economic, legal and cultural norms – as well as used wisely and compassionately, and not squandered. We are rapidly draining nature's capital, to put it in crass economic terms, which are the only terms most politicians and pundits and corporate elites seem to understand. We are racing towards ecological bankruptcy at an ever-accelerating rate, and will see our children live as beggars in an ocean of toxic waste if we don't change our course, and fast. Of course, most people – aside from the business and political elite – understand this by now. But awareness is not enough. It is high time for much more serious action.

> *"Climate change — human-made global warming — is happening. It is*
> *already having noticeable impacts…. If we stay on with business as usual,*
> *the southern U.S. will become almost uninhabitable…. It is time for all of*
> *us to get Tea-Party-angry about what our political system has become and*
> *about the intergenerational injustice being perpetrated on young people."*
>
> *– James Hansen, NASA's leading climatologist*

Addressing the present and rapidly escalating environmental crisis which humanity undeniably faces will require more of us than a simple act of recycling or "buying green." It will require, above all, a restoration and a renewal of democracy – a reclaiming of democracy from the ruling and highly pathological corporate elite. We must reclaim our democracy, or the earth will not be a habitable place for any human beings to live, in just a few short decades or less. If you want a future for humanity on this planet, reclaim your democracy now, or there will be none. This is the reality of our time. Let us do what needs to be done.

Why don't we have a massive infusion of investment of public funds in clean, renewable energy? Because the big oil, gas and coal companies don't want it: they are profiting from the status quo, they have a vested interest in the status quo, so the answer is an emphatic, "No." If we shifted the subsidies that are presently given out to the oil, gas and coal giants, and put it into clean, renewable solar, wind, co-generation and geothermal energy instead, we would be making rapid progress, by leaps and bounds every year, not only in greening our energy and transportation systems and becoming a truly sustainable society, but also in terms of energy self-reliance, economic strength and job creation. But Exxon and company have our politicians by the, um, purse strings: and so they pull the strings, and we the people, as well as the earth, lose out.

Why are we the people being treated as guinea pigs while the earth is being treated as a laboratory, when hundreds of responsible scientists have warned

that genetically engineered foods and crops pose serious and largely unfore-
seeable dangers to human health and the environment, and that such practices are unethical, irresponsible, highly imprudent, highly reckless and
highly dangerous? The majority of people are rightly wary about genetically
modified food and crops, and are generally opposed to these: but the biotech
giants have the clout in our political arenas; they pull the purse strings of our
politicians, and so, what big money wants, big money gets – democracy and
the people be damned.

Why don't we shift our tax system from taxing employment, through payroll taxes, which works directly against job creation, and also shift the tax
burden off small and medium businesses, the poor and the middle class, and
instead tax pollution, thus easing the burden on the majority of families and
businesses while creating incentives to pollution reduction? We don't have
sane and effective, just and fair, environmentally sensible tax laws because
while this would benefit the great majority of the people, create jobs and economic vitality, help clean up the environment and steer us in the direction
of true sustainability – while improving the quality of our air, soil, food and
water and also strengthening small business – it is not what the corporate
giants want. So again, it is a no go.

Why do we not have a significant smog tax for vehicles that get less than
40mpg, and equally significant government rebates for vehicles that get
better than 50mpg or have ultra-low or zero emissions? Because this would
require the auto industry and the car manufacturing giants to improve their
standards, and worse, it would mean that the oil companies wouldn't make
their usual obscenely stratospheric profits. Big oil and big auto says no, so
again, this is a no-go, and the politicians defer as usual to their masters.

Why do we have massive farm subsidies benefiting mainly the agribusiness, petrochemical, biotech and junk food giants, and an escalating war on
organic farming? As Richard Heinberg has said, petro-chemical industrial
agriculture has been nothing short of an ecological catastrophe – it is utterly
unsustainable. We need to shift to clean, healthy and sustainable organic
agriculture en mass, and as rapidly as possible, just as we need to reduce our
fossil fuel consumption and switch to clean, renewable energy. But do we
see a shift in the multi-billion dollar subsidies anywhere on the horizon? No,

we do not, and the reason we do not is that the current government policies benefit the petrochemical, biotech, agribusiness and processed food giants. Monsanto, McDonalds, Nestle and Kraft are making a killing on the existing system, quite literally as well as figuratively, and if they say no, our political elites say, "Ok boss – whatever you say." Poison the people and the planet, just don't cut off my re-election financing.

Why was the US Environmental Protection Agency gutted over the past decade? Because that is what big business wanted, and what big business wants, big business gets – at least unless and until we the people reclaim our democracy, and push back the vested interests of the corporate elite so that democracy can function, and not simply be a hollow shell run by and for the ruling business elite, with little more than a rubber stamp action on the part of the bought and paid for political elite.

It is not widely known, but it is a fact: when the tar sands are counted, and the exaggerated claims of the Saudi reserves are corrected for accuracy, Canada has the largest remaining oil reserves in the world. And while Canada is rapidly expanding its environmentally devastating oil extraction from the tar sands and plans for a new pipeline are being laid to suck the black gold from out under the people's feet, and the oil companies are raking in many billions of dollars a year in profits, why is it that it is unspeakable and unthinkable to charge a fair and just price for the extraction by these companies in the form of royalty payments made to the Canadian people? (The tar sands project should be killed – oil extraction royalties are a separate issue.) When certain Scandinavian countries charge $8 a barrel in extraction fees, paid as royalties to the people of the land, and Canada charges less than a dollar a barrel – while massively subsidizing the already profitable oil giants – something is clearly awry. Why is it that a fair price for extraction of a public resource, a resource of the commons, a resource that belongs to the people, paid to the people in return for the very lucrative opportunity to carry off this national treasure to whomever will pay the highest price abroad, is an utterly inexpressible, unutterable thought, and nary a word is whispered of this most obvious and patently just and sensible notion by the political elite or the mass media?

The answer is as clear as the profits are exorbitant: big oil dominates the capital and the political process, and none dare speak the truth that stares us daily in the face, let alone challenge the situation and right the wrong. Raising the extraction rates by seven dollars a barrel would still leave the oil companies with large, fat profits, although admittedly, the tar sands might be less lucrative, and possibly not feasible economically for some few years, until the price of oil rises further on the world stage, as it will. Such a modest and completely justified increase in extraction rates, as decided upon and enacted by a democratic government of the people, by the people, for the people, would flood the public coffers with funds, making ample money available for the development and creation of a clean and green, renewable energy and transportation system for the nation, as well as for social programs such as health care, education, day care and affordable housing. But while this should be an obvious and immediate step that is taken at once to bolster funding for a transition to a green and just society as well as the funding of much loved and overwhelmingly popular social programs, it is not even possible to mention the idea without immediately being excommunicated from the mainstream political discourse, raising the fevered ire of the corporate elite, and possibly risking a burning at the stake. Oil companies rule this fair and gentle land of the North, and once again, the people and the earth be damned.

Why do we not have a massive and much-needed investment by governments in green infrastructure, creating not just the groundwork and foundation for an ecological society, but truly enormous job creation and economic stimulus in the process, launching continent-wide energy-efficient light rail, mass transit networks and a clean, renewable solar-hydrogen infrastructure? California put in place the first leg of a hydrogen highway, at a cost of $100 million. For under $20 billion we could have a zero-emission, clean, renewable solar-hydrogen fuel and transportation network that spans all of North America – this may sound like a lot of money, and it is, but it is just 10% of the annual cost of maintaining the imperial wars in the Middle East and North Africa. The money spent on the wars in Iraq and Afghanistan alone have now cost over $2.5 trillion. That is approximately 100 times the amount needed to build a zero-emission, clean, renewable, energy self-reliant solar-hydrogen infrastructure for the entire continent of North America.

The U.S. federal government has admitted that over $1.2 trillion goes missing every year into black ops – Congress is unable to trace it, but it is acknowledged. Get rid of the military-industrial complex and the CIA and there will be over $1.5 trillion a year for green infrastructure, environmental protection and remediation, and also funds to help the rapidly sinking great majority of the American people and create jobs through such green infrastructure projects.

Why don't we have an enormous and urgently needed green infrastructure program right now? Because vested interests oppose it – because the Wall Street kleptocrats and their political allies have pillaged the nation to the extent that the country is now on the brink of bankruptcy, and more importantly, because the corporate elite insist upon ongoing, astronomically expensive and murderous wars for oil and other natural resources, thus entailing an absolute paucity of funds for anything that matters in terms of ecological sanity or human well-being. Bringing the troops home and ending wars for oil and other natural resources would save more than enough to build a continent-wide clean and renewable, green transportation infrastructure, massively stimulating the economy and creating millions of jobs in the process – and it would still leave many hundreds of billions a year left over for funding schools, health care and other human needs. But we don't have a green transportation infrastructure on the table, because this is not what the big oil, gas, coal, automotive and military-industrial giants want. Again, the people and the earth lose, because money rules over our politics, and not common sense, human decency or environmental sensibility, or even basic sanity.

Why do we still have millions of people dying and being killed in wars for oil and other resources, bankrupting the country and draining off critically needed funds that could and should be used to create a green economy and infrastructure, employing millions of people in the process, and pulling the people out of a financial and economic tail-spin? Because the oil and military-industrial complex corporate giants want it this way, and the people and the earth can go to hell, as far as they are concerned – and because Wall Street dictates the policies of Washington, Ottawa, Paris and London. If we want a green economy, a full employment economy, a just economy, an end to poverty, an end to imperial wars, or a future for our children, we will have to wrest control over our democracy from the corporate elite who now dominate it and severely limit and constrain our policy choices. This is the simple fact of the matter.

Our financially dependent political elite are in the pockets of the oil, gas, coal, biotech, agribusiness, petrochemical and other corporate giants, so policies and programs that are good for the environment and for the people are just not on the table – regardless of whether they would be good for human well-being, regardless of whether they would stimulate the economy and create jobs, regardless if they are arguably necessary for human life to continue beyond the next couple of decades on this planet, and regardless of whether the majority of the people want them – which they do. The great majority of people now want stronger environmental policies, programs and legislation – as well as peace, social justice and meaningful democracy, human rights and civil liberties. The corporate giants do not, so the people get the shaft. This is not about being anti-business; it is about democratic control of our environmental policies and programs, our economy and the commons, for the benefit of all. Corporate influence is in the way. The corporate elite are the barricade in the hall. They must be moved aside – and firmly if necessary.

You don't have to be anti-business to be opposed to corporate rule, by the way; to be opposed to rule by corporate elites is simply to favour democracy – and frankly, to call it as it is: to oppose fascism. Corporatism, as Mussolini himself defined, is the merger of business with the state. Anyone who values freedom or democracy must therefore oppose corporatism: which is the unchecked power of business elites, and an empire of corporate dominance over all aspects of society, including the economy, politics, culture and the media. To be anti-corporatist is not to be anti-business: it is simply to understand that any form of unchecked power invariably leads to tyranny and the destruction of freedom; and therefore, to be opposed to such unchecked powers by any kind of elite.

You don't have to be anti-business to oppose the take-over of democratic government by business elites – you simply have to be sane. You can be pro-business and anti-corporatist: and anyone who truly values democracy must, of logical and practical necessity, be anti-corporatist, regardless of their views on business.

I am belabouring the point because the corporate-owned and dominated media repeatedly portray any kind of critique of unchecked corporate powers as leftist lunacy. Here is breaking news for anyone who still buys into this red-scare propaganda that lingers from the McCarthy era, like a can of rotting tuna stinking up the entire house and driving the people to nausea and revulsion: people on the right and the left and in the centre politically are, by an overwhelming majority, in favour of constitutional democracy, and opposed to any kind of dominance over the democratic political process by any kind of elite, including the now globally dominant business elite.

"There has been a corporate takeover of politics. You have something called ALEC—the American Legislative Exchange Council—where corporations literally will pay huge sums of money to get together with politicians, draft model legislation that is then put across the US through state legislation, which is easier to pass than federal legislation."

– Global Comment writer Anna Lekas Miller

"America's political classes would do well to listen to the grievances of those involved with Occupy Wall Street, for they undoubtedly represent a set of anxieties shared by a great deal of the population. The corporate take-over of the American political process has not gone unnoticed, neither has the disparity between continued Wall Street profits and the cuts to the welfare state. As unemployment continues at high numbers, resentment surely stirs among those whose lives are slowly being drained at the expense of the corporate state. Recently, New York mayor Michael Bloomberg warned that there would be riots in the streets if Washington does not create more jobs, warning of an American Arab Spring."

– Emily Manuel, In These Times

Where once we had to wrest power from the church, the monarchy and the aristocracy who were overstepping their bounds, in order to secure democracy, human rights, equality and freedom, we now must wrest power from an unwieldy and overbearing, frankly tyrannical and self-serving business elite – and everybody who is in the least way sane and rational, who is not neck-deep in denial and who hasn't been living under a rock for the past fifty years, knows it.

Support for constitutional democracy and checks on corporate power, and the resultant or concomitant opposition to corporate rule, now cuts across the political spectrum. The people are no longer fooled by the red-scare tactics, nor by the broader corporate spin which seeks to mask the obvious: the emperor has no clothes, and everybody knows it – corporations have usurped democratic political powers, and are far over-stepping their proper bounds. Conservatives, liberals, libertarians and progressives alike now understand this, and know this quite viscerally – and are rightly concerned and rapidly running out of patience in the face of an intolerable situation of corporate oligarchy that seeks limitless powers for itself, while undermining every human value and endangering our very survival on this earth.

We now have grassroots populist conservatives such as Ron Paul and Alex Jones, along with Texas Republicans and the Main Street Alliance of Small Business Owners saying the same thing as progressives and people on the left: corporations are out of control, pillaging the nation and the planet, threatening democracy and running rampant – and they need to be reigned in; the people must reclaim their democracy. It is clear now that what I had called for four years ago, which is a coalition of the grassroots, a new union of the people to restore democracy, is not only feasible – it is being born. And that is precisely what we need now.

The reality, which virtually everyone knows, is that the democratic governments of the world are now in hoc, in debt, in dependency and in servitude to a globally dominant international business elite; and virtually all of the major political parties are now the servile lackeys to the ruling corporate empire. Meanwhile, the people increasingly see through this whole pathetic charade, and are becoming quite fed up with it.

You don't have to lean toward the left politically to be opposed to corporate rule: and at the level of the grassroots, people from the right and the left, conservatives, liberals and progressives, are now beyond wary of unchecked corporate powers – and wish to see democracy reclaimed by the people. What is needed now is a coalition of all those who favour democracy over corporate empire and corporate rule. This is beginning to emerge, and none too soon.

The suicidal kleptocracy of our presently reigning global order of neo-feudal corporatism must end – and now, before we extinguish ourselves from this small and beautiful, fragile, little blue planet. Democracy must be restored: and with power returned to the people, where it rightfully belongs, the commons can once again be protected and shared, wisely and judiciously, for the benefit of all, and for a better future for all humankind.

If we wish for survival, for a future worth living, or for any future for our children and the children of the earth, then it is absolutely necessary that democracy be reclaimed by the people. This is the most urgent necessity of the time. If Thomas Paine, Thomas Jefferson, Abraham Lincoln, George Washington or Voltaire were alive today, they most assuredly would be urging it. We should heed their call, the call of their distant but ever-near voices of reason and common sense, and reclaim our power. Restore democracy now. Bring the power back to the people, and let us begin again.

Let it begin. The great turning is here. A new renaissance is being born. Let us work together to bring about a better future and a better world for all. The power is in our hands. We must simply own it, and acknowledge that it is ours.

We have run out of time for idle chit-chat, partisan zealotry and pleasant euphemisms, for polite evasiveness and meek avoidance of the realities that we face. Let us now renew and reclaim our democracy: and we shall in the process, and by this means only, renew and reclaim the commons, for the common good of all. It is this, or it is a dark age ahead – make no mistake. Make your choice wisely. Our future, and our children's future, depend upon the choices we make now.

Be bold I say, and let us reclaim our future, and the future of humanity – if not for ourselves, then most certainly and assuredly for the sake of the children of this earth. Their lives and their future cannot be written off, even if we are willing to write off our own. Act now.

"The other superpower" is beginning to stir: humanity is beginning to awaken. And nothing, no reactionary force, can stop the rising tide of an awakened humanity. The future is in our hands. I urge all of us now to embrace that power, and to act together to reclaim our future and our world, by first reclaiming our democracy and our power.

Unite now, and let us restore democracy to its proper place – in the hands of the people. Our future and our children's future hangs in the balance. Let us not hesitate now – we cannot afford to do so. Let us begin, or begin again with renewed energy and a deepened commitment: for we *shall* succeed, and humanity *shall* have a new day.

> *"We must all hang together, or assuredly, we shall all hang separately....*
> *United we stand, divided we fall."*
>
> – *Benjamin Franklin*

> *"It is within our power now to begin the world anew."*
>
> – *Thomas Paine*

As Arundhati Roy so eloquently and beautifully put it, another world is not only possible: she is already being born. Go now – reflect, read, ponder and discuss: then let us act together to bring about a new day for humanity and this earth. I urge you, act now. It is not too late, and what we do or fail to do now, will decide our future, and the future of humanity.

Above all, unite the people to reclaim their democracy. This is the most pivotal and most urgent of tasks at hand. Unite now, and let democracy reign!

The people *will* reclaim their power. It has already begun. The writing is on the wall. The corporate empire – the last of a series of empires that have risen and fallen through the past five thousand years of history, the clay feet that David spoke of – is teetering and about to fall. It is a wounded and dying, and still yet a dangerous beast, to be sure, but this latest of empires is now crumbling – even while it flails madly in its death throes to preserve its life and maintain its power, and flaunts its power with brazen disregard and sheer contempt for humanity, democracy and life on earth. Its legitimacy is destroyed, by its own acts of malfeasance and abuse of power; and it is only a matter of time before its final demise. The people should see and clearly recognize the opportunity, and reclaim their power and their democracy now.

Rise now and unite. It is time for the full flowering of democracy, and the healing of this fair earth. Unite! And let us take back our democracy, for the benefit of all, and for the future of all life on earth, including our own children, and our children's children. The time has come for a new dawn.

JTR
September 28, 2011
S.D.G.